D1551990

8790

Just for nice : German-Canadian folk art / edited by
Magnús Einarsson and Helga Benndorf Taylor. --
Hull, Quebec : Canadian Museum of Civilization,
c1993.
124 p. : ill.

Includes bibliographical references.
06894852   ISBN:0660140098 (pbk.)

1. Art, German - Canada - Exhibitions. 2. Ethnic art -
Canada - Exhibitions. 3. Germans - Canada - Social life
and customs - Exhibitions. 4. Folk art - Canada -
(SEE NEXT CARD)

Just for Nice

GERMAN-CANADIAN FOLK ART

EDITED BY
MAGNÚS EINARSSON AND HELGA BENNDORF TAYLOR

CANADIAN MUSEUM OF CIVILIZATION

© 1993 Canadian Museum of Civilization

CANADIAN CATALOGUING IN PUBLICATION DATA

Canadian Museum of Civilization
Just for nice: German-Canadian folk art
Issued also in French under the title: Un brin de fantaisie
ISBN 0-660-14009-8

1. Art, German — Canada — Exhibitions.
2. Ethnic art — Canada — Exhibitions.
3. Germans — Canada — Social life and
customs — Exhibitions. 4. Folk art —
Canada — Exhibitions. I. Einarsson, Magnús.
II. Benndorf, Helga. III. Title.
IV. Title: German-Canadian folk art.

FC106.G3C32 1993   971.'00431   C93-099440-X
F1035.G3C32 1993

PRINTED IN CANADA

Published by the
Canadian Museum of Civilization
Hull, Quebec
J8X 4H2

Project coordinator:
Catherine Cunningham-Huston

Text editor:
Heather Ebbs

Design:
Purich Design Studio

Production:
Deborah Brownrigg

Photography:
Richard Garner photographed most of the objects from the collections.

Harry Foster photographed the objects on the following pages:
pp. 42, 48 (top), 56 (top left),
66 (bottom), 87 (on the right),
90 and 100.

Other photographs:
©Karsh, Ottawa, p. 7
Richard Henning Field, pp. 13-17
David J. Goa, p. 20
Wesley C. Mattie, p. 23

Cover:
Panel from wooden chest

Back cover:
Wooden chest; model church

Contents

Contents *continued*

©KARSH, OTTAWA

EDWARD SCHREYER

I was delighted when Magnús Einarsson asked me to write this foreword. It will soon be one hundred years since the day my family arrived in Canada from Bingen on the Rhine. For a hundred years before that, my family had lived in the easternmost reaches of Galicia in the old Austrian Empire.

When my grandfather reached Manitoba a century ago, there were few organized municipalities and school districts outside Winnipeg. The land was raw frontier, and the basics of local self-government and education were still almost entirely lacking. This was due to change soon, however, and with a rush.

Nevertheless, even by the 1870s, there were already significant communities of German-speaking Canadians in certain parts of Canada. Indeed, ever since Hans Bernhardt registered some arpents of farmland near the village of Québec in the seventeenth century, there has been a steady increase of Canadians who identify with the traditions of the German language and culture.

It is a matter of both historical interest and powerful nostalgia to read here about the founding of Lunenberg County in Nova Scotia in the eighteenth century, and about the migration of large numbers of Pennsylvania Deutsch between 1780 and 1810. It was from this group that our recently deceased former Governor General Roland Michener was descended. It is equally interesting to note that the major centre of the German presence in Canada from the 1800s to 1914 was the area of Kitchener-Waterloo, Ontario (and that the principal mover and founder of Ontario Hydro early in this century, Sir Adam Beck, lived in this same community).

The German communities of Ontario had frequent visits from the royal family of that era, largely because Queen Victoria and her immediate family were direct descendants of several generations of German-speaking parentage.

Farther west, the immigration of several thousand Mennonites in the 1870s to the areas centring on Steinbach and Altona was followed by the beginnings of large-scale German immigration from central and eastern Europe. By the 1890s, Winnipeg's German-speaking community was large enough to sustain a newspaper and a formally incorporated society.

Behind all this history must surely be a diversity of individual hopes, accomplishments and, yes, anxieties as well. Certainly, individually and collectively, this community has contributed directly and consistently to the history of Canada's growth from frontier colony to nation. But what were the folk ways, the techniques, the tools, the furnishings and the objects of art that these people brought with them or created here?

These questions, which are treated in this book, are an important parallel to the history that has been researched and published. The Canadian Museum of Civilization is to be commended for its initiative in publishing this volume, which complements its exhibition **"Just for Nice": German-Canadian Folk Art.**

Generally speaking, Canadians of German ancestry have blended so well into the Canadian fabric as to become indistinguishable within a very few years. That is not to say, however, that they should lose their interest in the history of their ancestors' contribution to an earlier Canada. It is an impressive story that deserves to be recalled and appreciated. This book will help to achieve exactly that.

Ed Schreyer

EDWARD SCHREYER
GOVERNOR GENERAL OF CANADA (1979–1984)

CURATORIAL NOTE

MAGNÚS EINARSSON

CURATOR, NORTH EUROPEAN PROGRAMME
CANADIAN CENTRE FOR FOLK CULTURE STUDIES

Back in the summer of 1974, a colleague was standing with a Mennonite farmer inside his barn near Vineland in southern Ontario. High up in one of the gables he noticed a design that had been cut out of the boards, letting in shafts of light in the pattern of a star. He asked the farmer whether this was a hex sign of some sort, placed there perhaps for protection of the animals or to ensure a good crop. The farmer replied in the negative, saying, "It's just for pretty." This phrase is a variant of a much-used Ontario (Pennsylvania) German saying, "Just for nice," or sometimes even "Pretty for nice." The casualness of the expression and its delivery, however, belie the significance of its underlying message; namely, that beauty ("pretty") is an important part of one's environment, even in the humdrum, workaday world, even in a place where, most of the time, only beasts are there to appreciate it.

The evidence of this kind of conscious artistry permeates the traditional communities of Germanic Canada. Whether it is in the older communities of eastern Canada with their highly decorative styles, rich colours, symmetry and traditional motifs, or in the western communities where expressive presentation is more apparent in spareness, order and plainness, there is a clear and pervasive sense of the desire to make one's environment as comely as possible. The reasons are many: tradition, habit, something to do during the winter months and, simply, the need to please the eye, one's own and others'. (A well-known Ontario (Pennsylvania) German expression is "This I could put in my eye.") But there is a sense here also, especially in the religious communities, which are the primary carriers of these visual traditions, that the one who is ultimately being pleased is omnipresent, all-seeing God. Prettiness, like cleanliness and tidiness, acknowledges and affirms religious faith. This has given German-Canadian folk art a vitality that has ensured not just its survival, but its continuity and growth through generation after generation. By no means, however, has it remained creatively static.

German-Canadian folk art has undergone many changes over the generations. ("German" in this publication refers to German culture as found in the traditional homelands of Germany, Austria and Switzerland as well as in diverse other German communities such as those in eastern Europe and Canada.) Many objects of daily use in the various homelands were abandoned when the time came to move to Canada. Other objects were taken along and kept until they fell apart, and then abandoned or, if replaced, often adapted to suit changed circumstances. New materials were introduced (often softwood for hardwood), design and decoration were simplified, new uses were found for old objects and,

sometimes, traditional decoration was applied to new objects. But until relatively recently, the traditional aesthetic framework generally stayed intact.

More fundamental changes are happening now. I will mention just two. The first and most important one to have overtaken the artistic output of these communities, eastern and western, is individualism. Since at least the end of the nineteenth century, folk artists have increasingly turned their attention away from community tastes and traditional dictates and responded to stimuli from the larger, surrounding, mainstream culture. Several readily observable changes, because of the historical depth of German folk-art expression in this country, stand out dramatically against the background of folk or community art of earlier periods. Realistic representation, whether based on observation, personal experience, history or fantasy, has replaced abstract decoration and, largely, the use of traditional motifs and symbols. Contemporary popular art has also been freed from instrumental functionality and has found, instead, an outlet in freestanding objects made for the purpose of record, whimsy, criticism or humour. This freedom has also, alas, meant the abandonment of precision, and sometimes skill, for the sake of free expression. The artist's pleasure in this modern type of popular art is no longer in delivering a well-crafted and tightly interpreted variant of the expected and traditional, but in evocation, surprise and even shock. What communalism remains is found in the more or less realistic representations of shared experiences within the home-community, or in the home-community as it was. The works of Jacob Roth and Henry Pauls are a case in point. Their works are an expression of sentiment and longing for what used to be, and in this sense the artists are transitional figures between the old and the new.

The other change is also related to a sentimental desire to recapture the past. This revivalist art tends to be characterized by a deliberate, studied and ultrafaithful rendition of some original work or type of work, which, paradoxically, is often combined with the exaggeration of its original dimensions, either enlargement or miniaturization. Another characteristic associated with these objects is their placement in the home or community; they are usually given a place of honour or visual prominence, where, as ethnic icons, they give comfort and a sense of continuity to people whose ties to their culture and community have become tenuous. Often, however, revival art is driven as much by commerce as by sentiment. There is little of this type of work in our collections, but it is readily observable at folk and ethnic festivals and many tourist centres; there, it can be purchased (often, not by German-Canadians) and enjoyed simply for its own sake rather than any attendant feelings of ethnic loyalty. Revivalist art of this sort, whatever the intention behind its genesis, is an important segment of the Canadian folk-art scene, because it is tied up with the question of identity in a homogenizing world that increasingly insists equality can be represented only by sameness.

In a dynamic acculturative situation such as we have in Canada, folk art and lore help, for a good while, to shape, signal and sustain the cultural values of a given community, but it is in the long run that folk art, aside from its aesthetic affectivity and influence on "serious" art, proves its ultimate worth. Long, long after the inevitable has happened, after language is lost and culture irredeemably changed, folk art is a storehouse of motifs and imagery. It is a storehouse from which individuals can select identity symbols to anchor and ally themselves to a cultural heritage to which they otherwise have no real or meaningful access.

While these would seem to be the two principal directions that German-Canadian folk art is taking (as in most other ethnic groups), other changes are bound to occur as responses to now unforeseen developments. One thing folklorists now know, two hundred years after the brothers Grimm established the discipline, is that folklore is not an antiquarian pursuit; the forms of folk art (as well as folklore) are highly adaptive because they represent one of the most basic mechanisms by which ordinary people can deal creatively with change, especially the kind of radical change it takes to settle in a new country. The nature of some of these changes is documented in words and images in the following pages.

This volume is based solely on the collections of the Canadian Museum of Civilization (CMC), gathered for the last twenty-three years by staff of the Canadian Centre for Folk Culture studies. My first foray into this field to find German-Canadian artifacts was in 1971 to Galt (now Cambridge), Ontario, at the suggestion of Dr. George MacDonald (now the executive director of the CMC), who on his travels had spotted the magnificent oak trunk shown on page 40. On that baptismal trip I also found the Lind chest shown on page 40, and over the years my colleague Wes Mattie and I found many others. The German collection has grown to about a thousand items from every part of the country and relates to almost every aspect of German-Canadian rural life. For this volume, however, we selected only those items that most clearly reveal the German-Canadian expressive tradition in all its temporal, regional and religious variations.

Incidentally, with the exception of some eleventh-century Norse artifacts discovered at L'Anse aux Meadows in Newfoundland and others in the eastern Arctic, most of our oldest European artifacts are of German or Ontario (Pennsylvania) German origin. Germans were some of the first non-French settlers in almost all parts of Canada, but aside from that and aside from the great stability of our rural German communities, it is evident that these artifacts have lasted so long because, in addition to being well made, they are beautiful, making people want to continue to use them, care for them and pass them on to the next generation.

So far we have only a few hints of the kinds of long-term developments that German-Canadian folk art might undergo in future years. Because of its presence in Canada almost from the beginning of the country's settlement, it should prove to be interesting and fruitful to monitor those changes, especially in cities, where the struggle for identity is most acute. More attention also needs to be paid now to the postwar immigrant generation and their children. Many of our leading craftspeople and artists hail from this group.

The impact on German-Canadian culture is only one side of the coin. The most interesting thing to watch will be the long-term impact of German culture on our shared Canadian culture. Our most popular foods are the hamburger and the frankfurter; the Christmas tree is the centre of our most popular festival; and Oktoberfest is a part of life in many regions of the country. Ontario-German folk imagery and Amish buggies and dress are now as Canadian as maple syrup. The list will inevitably keep growing, yet most of us will not notice it happening. That, of course, is the ultimate sign of acceptance—when it becomes "ours" and not "theirs."

In one of the medieval Icelandic chronicles, *The Saga of the Greenlanders*, which recounts the first Norse journeys to North America in the eleventh century, the German-speaking Tyrkir comes across wild grapes. In response to this pleasant and unexpected discovery the leader of the expedition, Leifr Eiriksson, decides to name the country Vinland. (The Icelandic word for grapes is vinber, literally wineberries.) I have come to think of this as a particularly auspicious beginning for the presence of German culture on these shores. Because while their contributions in all aspects of Canadian life and culture are significant, their most enchanting and enduring legacy may prove to be their contribution to the arts, especially their folk arts, which for the last three hundred years have added a much-needed sense of *douceur* (sweetness) to Canadian life.

I would like to take this opportunity to thank our many contributors, all of them outstanding leaders in their field. Professor Hartmut Froeschle has written a much-needed historical overview of the German presence in Canada. It helps to make sense of the complicated immigration and settlement history of the many religious and cultural groups that make up the German-Canadian demographic profile. Dr. Richard Henning Field,

David Goa, Professor Nancy-Lou Patterson and Steve Prystupa have grounded their theoretical insights and observations in the realities of a specific cultural region or group, all of them providing new insights and information not previously available in print. My colleague at CMC, Dr. Robert B. Klymasz, has made an important observation on the use of text in German folk art, on the basis of a microanalysis of the work of a single artist, Henry Pauls. Dr. Helga Benndorf Taylor, my research associate on this project, has taken a more abstract approach, which reminds us of the Old World roots of German-Canadian folk art.

This volume has been a truly collaborative effort. So many people inside and outside the CMC have lent a helping hand that it becomes very difficult to name them all. A few, however, must be mentioned: Susan Bourke, Joseph Schneider Haus, Kitchener; Tim Campbell, Canadian Museum of Contemporary Photography; Elisabeth Froeschle, Toronto; Dr. Art Grenke, National Archives of Canada; Chris Huntington, Mahone Bay, Nova Scotia; Claus C. Jobes and Dieter Kiesewalter of the German-Canadian Congress; Ilse Lindemann, Embassy of the Federal Republic of Germany, as well as Dr. Robert McGhee and Dr. Stephen Inglis of the CMC.

Only their help, forbearance and generosity have made this project possible. *Vielen Dank.*

German Influences on Lunenburg County Material Life and Folk Art

Richard Henning Field

We Canadians see ourselves as living in a country of many solitudes, a mix of language and ethnic tradition. The change and adaptation people must make to a new environment were as important to eighteenth-century Europeans arriving in the New World as they are for the immigrants arriving today.

The various factors determining assimilation in the past, however, were different from those faced by today's newcomers. Physical and climatic elements were the most difficult and challenging obstacles to deal with. How they confronted these obstacles often meant the difference between life and death, between the survival of a settlement and its disappearance. As the newcomers met the challenge and established their societies in imitation of their homelands, the initial conservatism of eighteenth-century colonial society was altered by time, distance and the greater acceptance and control of the new environment.

The evolution of colonial culture was embodied in changing attitudes and assumptions that, in turn, found expression in the material traditions: in the buildings and objects made and used from first settlement to later generations. Eighteenth-century Nova Scotia is best understood as a colonial enterprise on the part of the English and French, and as an extension of European culture.

The arrival of the foreign Protestant German and Swiss European settlers to Nova Scotia under the auspices of the British government was part of this venture; another facet of the persistent point-counterpoint match played between France and England throughout the eighteenth century. German and Swiss settlers—European Protestants—were lured to the colony to counteract the Catholic influence of the French Acadians. This plan was not carried to full fruition by the British government; instead, in 1755, they expelled the Acadian population. The swift effect of this solution and the abandonment of the policy to colonize Nova Scotia with German settlers essentially forced the foreign Protestants into an extended period of cultural seclusion. These newcomers, who had founded the town of Lunenburg, were isolated from their European homeland—a segregated fragment lost in a pervasively English environment and an unfamiliar landscape. Their cultural, social and material traditions were not reinforced by further migrations of fellow country-men or women. Migration to Lunenburg did not mirror the European German settlement of Pennsylvania.

Without the support of continual migration, the Lunenburg Germans forged an identity that was distinct while still fitting into their new cultural environment. These colonial immigrants had to shift their political loyalties, create a new sense of space and belonging, cope with disruptions in deeply rooted patterns of life and face the trials and experiences of both migrating to and settling in a new land. The process strengthened the conservative nature of the immigrants. It forced them to seek within their common European heritage traditional cultural, social and material manifestations of who and what they were as individuals, families and a community.

The evolution of ethnic identification and assimilation revealed itself in two important ways. The first was in the types of furnishings used in the domestic household and considered traditional objects commonly found in European German material culture settings, both in Europe and in Pennsylvania; these objects included desks, tall-case clocks, beds and cupboards. The second was in the way these objects were constructed and decorated. In surviving Lunenburg County domestic interiors from the late eighteenth and early nineteenth century, it is not unusual to find hearts, stars, whorls, diamonds and matchstick reeding carved on built-in parlour and kitchen cupboards and fireplace mantels. These decorative elements also adorned freestanding objects of furniture such as chests and cupboards, as well as small personal accessories such as document boxes.

The question is how this eighteenth-century European decorative tradition continued to be manifested in architecture, domestic furnishings and personal objects in the nineteenth and twentieth centuries. The link between the eighteenth and early twentieth century is not as obvious as one might wish. However, there are enough connecting points to suggest just how the material and decorative conventions of the first ninety years of settlement continued to play an important role in the decorative traditions of later generations of Lunenburg Germans up to the Second World War.

There is little question that Lunenburg County remains Germanic. In many respects it is this European legacy that sets the tone and character of the people of Lunenburg and marks the architecture, artistic traditions and lifestyle of the town and county as different from the rest of the province. For example, there are still a noticeable *Deutsch* accent and lilt in the everyday speech of these German and Swiss descendants, particularly in settlements outside Lunenburg, such as Feltzen South and Kingsburg.[1] Lunenburg town and county retain the strong Protestant character and work ethic of the first settlers, and many German foods are still served, including sauerkraut and various sausages.

GERMAN-LANGUAGE BOOKS

Nowhere is the evidence of the direct link between the Lunenburg Germans and their European heritage more obvious than in the various religious texts (Bibles, catechisms, psalm books) still commonly found in Lunenburg County. Mostly in German and usually dating before

1820, the texts embody the Protestant faith of the settlers and the individual and collective persistence of German as the primary or secondary tongue. As direct connections to their homeland, they were important reminders of their common European traditions. This fact was not missed by Anthony Henry, who published many almanacs in German for the Halifax and Lunenburg communities after being appointed Queen's Printer in Halifax in 1788. Nonetheless, most of the German religious texts and almanacs in Lunenburg County were produced in Pennsylvania, either by Christopher Sauer (Sower) or by Henrich Miller. Many copies of Sauer's Bibles, catechisms and psalm books are still to be found in storage sheds and attics.

Christoph Sower I (Senior) began his career as a printer and publisher in 1738 with his publication of a broadside and the first successful German almanac published in America. A year later he initiated the first successful German newspaper. In 1743, Sower I published the first North American Bible in a modern European language. Several copies of this first Bible exist in Lunenburg, imported sometime after the original settlement in 1753.[2] By far the most common German-language Bibles still found in Lunenburg are the second and third editions of the Sower I Bible produced by Christoph's son, Christopher, in 1762 and 1776.

Beyond copies of the German Bible, a large body of religious literature is also found in the county, including biblical commentaries, discussions of doctrine ranging from catechisms to theological monographs, psalm books and hymnals. Works published by Sower II and Henrich Miller,

Figure 1. Hughey birth and baptismal record, after 1817. Crousetown, Lunenburg County, Nova Scotia. Watercolour, ink and pencil on paper, 33 x 20 cm. Collection of the Art Gallery of Nova Scotia.

Figure 2. Corkum birth and baptismal record, after 1826. Weatherby, Lunenburg County, Nova Scotia. Watercolour and ink on paper, 22.1 x 33.7 cm. Collection of the Nova Scotia Museum.

a German English printer in Pennsylvania, have surfaced in several private collections.

One of the most important aspects of these religious works and almanacs printed in the province or imported into Lunenburg County is their emphasis on illustrations. Although no serious research has been conducted on the relationship between these printed illustrations and the various decorative motifs used to adorn objects, household interiors or Fraktur, it seems obvious that some interrelationship must have existed. The importance of illustrations and printed iconography, particularly in religious works, to those who could not read or write must be considered, but unfortunately falls outside the parameters of this study.

FRAKTUR

Although several authors have noted the similarity between the type of Fraktur found in Lunenburg County and the illuminated manuscripts of New England, it is inaccurate to think that the indigenous Lunenburg County Fraktur is non-Germanic in origin and concept. Nothing could be further from the truth. In fact, Fraktur was produced well into the second quarter of the nineteenth century in Lunenburg County.

For example, the David Saul Seaburger birth record, dated 1827, is composed mostly of Fraktur script; its minimal decoration includes floral motifs and calligraphic devices. It is a simple record announcing the birth of David Seaburger of Rose Bay, Lunenburg County, a descendant of the Seeburgers who migrated from the Palatinate in Germany in 1750. It is not unlike at least seven other records with similar script and minimal decoration announcing the births of other children in Kingsburg, LaHave and Lunenburg itself. These records date from 1805 to 1832.[3]

The Henrich Moser record is created with cutout paper in the form of a circle of eight hearts set around a central hub. Dated 1812, it is essentially a personal lament over the despair felt by Moser on living in a foreign country. The text is in German, and the script is a simple Fraktur form. The use of cut paper to create a circle of hearts is also found in the Pennsylvania Fraktur tradition. Usually, the heart motif is used for the expression of love between individuals, not for the love of an individual for his homeland. This particular form of cutout and decorated Fraktur is common to European German folk art dating from the late eighteenth century.

The two most important Lunenburg County Frakturs are the Conrad Edward Hughey birth and baptismal record dated after 1817, and the Frederick Corkum birth and baptismal record dated after 1826 (figures 1 and 2). The Conrad Hughey birth record indicates that he was born on November 2, 1816, and was baptized five months later on April 3, 1817. His godparents were Conrad Getson and Elizabeth Himmelman. Frederick Corkum was born July 25, 1826, and baptized on August 8, 1826. His godparents were Frederick and Elizabeth Corkum. According to a note attached to the record, Corkum died on February 28, 1910.

Although unsigned, there is little doubt that the Hughey record and the Corkum record are by the same hand. Both have solid, multicoloured borders, almost identical Fraktur lettering and similar decorative devices. The motifs on the Hughey record are simpler and fewer than those on the Corkum record. The lettering and the tulip-like flower on the Hughey example leave little doubt about the Germanic heritage of both the family and the maker. The Corkum record is more complex and detailed in the overall decorative design, with more elaborate floral motifs and lettering.

The one aspect that almost all Lunenburg County Fraktur seems to have in common is the absence of animal and human figures incorporated into the design. Almost all the decoration is either floral or uses

Figure 3. George Jung (1770–1793) gravemarker, 1793. Slate. Lunenburg Cemetery, Lunenburg County, Nova Scotia.

various calligraphic abstract devices. The most notable exception to this rule is the remains of a record in which a multi-coloured bird perched on a sphere is incorporated into the decoration.[4]

There is little question that Lunenburg County Fraktur embodies the European Fraktur traditions of the original foreign Protestant settlers. The fact that many of the Fraktur examples found in Lunenburg date from the first quarter and beginning of the second quarter of the nineteenth century suggests that, for many descendants, the use of Fraktur to celebrate birth and baptism was a personal ethnic reminder of who and what they were. The similarity between Lunenburg and New England Fraktur is certainly explainable considering the pervasive English environment in which the foreign Protestants found themselves. Indeed, the mix of English and German decorative tradition is found throughout the Lunenburg German material record. The Germanic background of the families who executed this Fraktur leaves little doubt about their understanding of their heritage, a heritage that guided their personal and family loyalties and spiritual devotions.

GRAVEMARKERS

The heart and tulip, considered by many to be the signature motifs of the Pennsylvania Germans, have not been found to date on any Lunenburg County Fraktur. However, they were used as decorative devices on Lunenburg County gravestones. As with Fraktur, these stones date from the late eighteenth century up to the second quarter of the nineteenth century.

One of the earliest is the 1793 George Jung (1770–1793) marker, which has a carved heart surrounded by a floral motif (Figure 3). The Rebecca Elizabeth Meissner (1783–1802) stone in the Lunenburg Cemetery has the date 1803 surrounded by a large, incised heart and was completed seven months after her death. The Johan Eisenhauer (1733–1805) marker in the Bayview Cemetery, Mahone Bay, is dated 1805 and is one of the rare examples showing the tulip as a decorative motif.

What these three stones have in common is that they are markers either for original settlers (Johan Eisenhauer), or for first-generation children (Meissner and Jung) who were born in the settlement but died young. It does not seem unusual that markers used for these three people would contain heart and tulip decorative devices reflecting their Germanic heritage. It does raise the question of how many times these motifs were used on other objects, including Fraktur and gravestones, that have not survived into this century.

As with Fraktur, the European German traditions were continued in gravestone carving. The Cookmen stone marks the grave of an infant (Phillip Cookmen) and is dated 1848. Carved in a primitive manner, it incorporates a crosshatched heart as part of the decoration.

The persistence of German influences on Lunenburg County material life is most evident when one looks at the architectural details of domestic interiors, furnishings and accessories produced during the first three generations of settlement.

Figure 4. Parlour mantel, 1780–1800. Hamm house, Blockhouse, Lunenburg County, Nova Scotia. The paint in the parlour of this house is in the original (now oxidized) putty green-grey colour. Note the diamond motifs separated by matchstick reeding.

The Knaut-Rhuland house (1793) and the Zwicker house (1795–1800) in the town of Lunenburg have matchstick-reeded arches in the centre hallways. In the Ernst house in Blockhouse, all the woodwork in the two parlours is decorated with matchstick reeding in combination with corner fans and diamonds, while the Hamm house has reeding combined with diamonds and whorls on both the parlour fireplace mantel and the parlour cupboard (Figure 4).

In the mid-eighteenth century, a vast number of publications spread the doctrine of classical architecture throughout the English-speaking world. Despite the classicism of the exteriors and interiors of the Lunenburg houses (whether Georgian or Cape Cod in style), the architectural details used to embellish these interiors have a distinctive character of their own. For example, the mantels and cupboards incorporating Germanic motifs become independent designs combining a definite Germanic character within the framework of the overall classical English manner. This leads to a distinctive Lunenburg German vernacular architectural style. The understanding of this process is the key to recognizing Germanic elements not only within the architecture and decorative arts, but also in the furniture made and used in Lunenburg County.

ARCHITECTURAL INTERIORS

Though mostly limited to ornamental highlights within the English Georgian architectural style of the late eighteenth century, Lunenburg County architecture exhibits the same Germanic decorative motifs, including hearts, whorls, stars, diamonds and reeding, used in Lunenburg German decorative art. This is not to say that these architectural details were not used elsewhere; rather, it simply suggests that their occurrence in Lunenburg County is firmly rooted in time and place within the parameters of German settlement.

Many houses in the county incorporate these motifs into the interior architectural details. The motifs were used mostly to embellish parlour fireplace mantels and cupboards, woodwork, and hearth-room cupboards and mantels. Most of these houses date from between 1775 and 1820.

FURNITURE

Virtually no one has explored the possibility that the German influence on Lunenburg and even Nova Scotia furniture might be anything more than a minor theme in the English-influenced colonial arts of the province. This is not surprising considering that very little work has been carried out on any aspects of eighteenth-century material life in the province, let alone the foreign Protestants. The generally held view about eighteenth- and nineteenth-century furniture of the south shore and the province is that great urban and rural English-inspired (and Scottish- and Irish-inspired)

Figure 6. Work table, 1780–1800. Mahone Bay, Lunenburg County, Nova Scotia. Note the two-board top held together with a small spline visible at the edge of the boards. The robust legs are whittled from solid blocks of birch, and the skirt is moulded in eighteenth-century fashion. Whereabouts unknown.

Figure 7. Work table, 1770–1790. Lunenburg County, Nova Scotia. Note the "cupid's bow" shaped skirt on the end, and the drawer in the side. The top is held in place by two cleats and is removable, as in the Pennsylvania German examples. Private collection.

Figure 5. Dummy Nauss ladderback side chair, 1800–1840. Mahone Bay, Lunenburg County, Nova Scotia. The rush seat and red paint are both original. The top back slat and middle stretcher are both pegged with lemon-shaped, not square-shaped, heads, suggesting a maker familiar with northern European as opposed to English cabinetmaking traditions. Private collection.

furniture was made here. In some parts of the province (French shore, south shore), ethnic subcultures produced some interesting, "folky" kinds of furniture that were essentially aberrations of mainstream furniture styles. This perception effectively labels ethnic furniture and decorative arts and their makers as second-rate when compared to furniture produced in the English tradition by trained cabinetmakers. It is certainly this attitude that has deterred many would-be researchers from looking into this ethnic material and thus restricted our understanding of both the furniture and the people who transplanted their culture to new places.

Nevertheless, when the foreign Protestants arrived in Nova Scotia in 1751 and 1752, forty-five men listed their occupation as carpenter or joiner, representing a total of 117 family members. These Germans and Swiss who settled in an English province had the opportunity to select from the forms and styles of both cultures. Yet almost no recognition has been accorded the foreign Protestant craftsmen who worked in Halifax and Lunenburg. Their influence on English cabinetmakers and styles has never been considered a possibility. There is little doubt that some of the eighteenth-century furniture produced in Lunenburg exhibits strong English influences, but some pieces embody a mix of both cultures in style and construction techniques. To begin to unravel all the possibilities suggested by this mix is beyond the scope of this essay, and would, in any case, require many years of research to understand. However, certain preliminary findings can be discussed.

Unquestionably, the most commonly identified German furniture pieces in Lunenburg County are Frank and John Jung's (Young) ladderback chairs and the turned and painted spinning wheels they

Figure 9. Detail of chest, Figure 8.

Figure 8. Chest of drawers, 1800–1820. Lunenburg County, Nova Scotia. The chevron and straight-reeded inset diamond motifs are also incorporated into the architectural details of domestic interiors dating from the same period or earlier (see Figure 4). Private collection.

signed. The case of the Jung ladderbacks is most indicative of how attributions to specific makers are made on the basis of a single stylistic feature. These chairs are identified by a very specific finial shape, yet no signed examples have ever been found.

A similar example of feature-based attribution involves ladderback chairs attributed to "Dummy" Nauss (Figure 5). The name "Dummy" stems from the fact that the round posts, stretchers and legs of these chairs were whittled by hand; Nauss is referred to as a "dummy" supposedly because he did not have or know how to use a lathe. The use of whittling as a technique of working the normally turned parts of chairs and tables is not unknown in Lunenburg County, and may have set the precedent for later nineteenth-century and twentieth-century decorative folk art that is chip-carved and incised by small knives. For example, a work table found in Mahone Bay has shaped legs whittled round from solid blocks of birch (Figure 6). The legs are mortised and tenoned to a skirt that is moulded along the bottom edge in eighteenth-century fashion. The two-board top of the table is braced on the underside with large forged nails. Other work tables are not unlike those found in the Pennsylvania German tradition (Figure 7).[5]

To get into a state of mind that allows one to look for German aspects in Lunenburg County furniture and folk and decorative arts is not an easy matter. Beyond certain obvious aspects of surface treatment and decoration that are considered Germanic, such as painted, incised or carved compass stars or diamonds, most of the features that betray the hands of a German craftsman are found in the details, or are hidden from view. Moreover, many of these techniques are found in other parts of the province. But even if pieces look stylistically like the work of an English cabinetmaker, an English cabinetmaker would not make it with Germanic techniques unless he had trained in this tradition. According to Benno Forman, "We have been taught to believe that a non-English maker of a piece of furniture in America must invariably betray himself because the proportions and details of his work will differ from the proportions, execution and details of work done by a craftsman trained in the English manner."

In discussing German influences on Pennsylvania furniture, Forman examines construction methods to identify furniture made by German craftsmen even though the style and aesthetic appearance may be English. Wedged dovetails, through tenons, double-wedged tenons and lemon-shaped pins (as in the Dummy Nauss chairs) are construction techniques all found in Lunenburg County that suggest German, or at least northern European, furniture traditions as opposed to the Anglo-American school.

All these observations about Lunenburg County furniture made using German methods of woodworking and construction are preliminary and require deeper study. There is little doubt, however, that when the

German joiners and turners landed in Lunenburg they were influenced by their stay in Halifax, and many produced English-style furniture.

One piece of furniture that combines an English style with bold Germanic decoration and colour is the chest of drawers in figures 8 and 9. The style is Hepplewhite, but the Germanic decorations include multireeded mouldings around each drawer, between drawers and around the entire outside edge of the front and sides. Each drawer front has matchstick-reeded diamonds, some with a chevron pattern and others simply vertical in design. The surface paint is the original combination of red and black. The drawer configuration is rare but not unknown in Nova Scotia. The matchstick and reeded decorations on this chest are identical to architectural details found in the reeded arch in the centre hall of the Knaut-Rhuland house, the chevron matchstick-reeded arch of the Zwicker house, the woodwork in the two parlours of the Ernst house and the parlour mantel and cupboard of the Hamm house. This is an important piece of Lunenburg County furniture; it warrants further research into origins of ownership and a search for similar examples.

SUMMARY

There exist in Lunenburg County two distinctive aspects that identify decorative art, folk art and furnishings as Germanic. One is the variety of decorative motifs and designs used to embellish everything from gravemarkers to family records to furniture to architectural interiors and accessories; the other is the construction and woodworking techniques used in cabinetmaking. In addition, one must also consider that many objects of folk or decorative art produced from the founding of the town to almost the present day were objects created by individuals who had little or no formal training as carpenters, cabinetmakers, turners or joiners. There is still much research to be conducted on the relationship between the trained and untrained artisan and how the two groups may have interacted and influenced each other.[6]

These features of Lunenburg material life were born from the interaction between the English and German decorative traditions and the resulting tensions and mix between these two groups. The same process is evident in Pennsylvania.

The development of nineteenth- and twentieth-century folk art is rooted in the Germanic decorative and woodworking traditions transferred from Europe by the foreign Protestants. During their stay in Halifax it was tempered by some English influence, but once settlers were in Lunenburg their folk art was maintained and perpetuated by the generations that followed. Lunenburg County did not lose its strong Germanic European heritage until the beginning of the Second World War.

To date, most scholars recognize Lunenburg County folk and decorative art because of the surface treatment or decoration. However, this is only part of the picture. A full study of construction and woodworking techniques and the origin of certain decorative motifs is long overdue. The existence of Germanic traditions in Lunenburg County cannot be denied, and it makes one wonder what influence these traditions had on the material life in other parts of the province.

NOTES

1. The German language did not disappear from Lunenburg County in the early nineteenth century as some might believe. German was still being spoken during the 1930s and early 1940s, until the rise of fascism in Germany and the Second World War. At the same time, many German books dating from the eighteenth century were destroyed, and objects incorporating various forms of the swastika into their decorative elements (such as hooked rugs and sailcloth mats) were burned.

2. I have seen three copies of the Sower I Bible, in various states of preservation, belonging to private families in Lunenburg.

3. I have examined all these records. Several for the Corkum family are by the same hand and executed in a deep brown ink, faded over time. They are decorated with floral motifs and calligraphic devices. All these records remain in private hands.

4. This record, found in a trunk in a house in Lunenburg County, was so far deteriorated that the family name was missing. With the lack of interest in works of art on paper, one wonders just what Fraktur has been lost and what remains still to be found buried in old books and trunks. Such items may be destroyed without ever seeing the light of day.

5. Tables with box or H-stretchers, turned or tapered/square legs, a single drawer (usually in one side), and a moulded and shaped skirt (usually in the form of a cupid's bow) have turned up in Lunenburg County, generally in poor states of preservation. Most of these tables, which probably date from the last quarter of the eighteenth century, are constructed with through mortises and forged nails. Although no one has made a specific study of them, these tables are among the most characteristic pieces of German-style furniture in Lunenburg County.

6. Much of the problem with our understanding of folk art in general is that it is often considered the product of individuals working from within themselves to create something. Yet, one cannot remove the makers from the social and cultural context, any more than one can remove them from their material context. Obviously, the cabinetmaker

who made the chest in Figure 9 was aware of the work of housewrights who were using similar types of decoration. It simply is not feasible that individual artisans or groups of craftsmen worked in isolation from each other. This topic requires further research.

BIBLIOGRAPHY

Bell, Winthrop. *The "Foreign Protestants" and the Settlement of Nova Scotia.* Toronto: University of Toronto Press, 1961.

Bird, Michael, and Terry Kobayashi. *A Splendid Harvest: Germanic Folk and Decorative Arts in Canada.* Toronto: Van Nostrand Reinhold, 1981.

Field, Richard Henning. "The Material Lives of Lunenburg German Merchants and Yeomen: The Evidence Based on Probate Inventories, 1760–1830." PhD thesis, Dalhousie University, 1990.

Forman, Benno M. "German Influences in Pennsylvania Furniture." In *Arts of the Pennsylvania Germans.* Ed. Scott Swank. New York: W.W. Norton, 1983.

Schlee, Ernst. *German Folk Art.* New York: Kodansha, 1980.

Sommer, Frank H. "German Language Books, Periodicals, and Manuscripts." In *Arts of the Pennsylvania Germans.* Ed. Scott Swank. New York: W.W. Norton, 1983.

Swank, Scott. "Proxemic Patterns." In *Arts of the Pennsylvania Germans.* Ed. Scott Swank. New York: W.W. Norton, 1983.

Weiser, Frederick. "Fraktur." In *Arts of the Pennsylvania Germans.* Ed. Scott Swank. New York: W.W. Norton, 1983.

Whitelaw, Marjory. *First Impressions: Early Printing in Nova Scotia.* Halifax: Nova Scotia Museum, 1987.

Young, Deborah A. *A Record for Time.* Halifax: Art Gallery of Nova Scotia, 1985.

For the Eyes of God Alone: The Meaning of the Hutterian Brethren Aesthetic

David J. Goa

There is a good deal about beauty in the Bible. The loveliness of creation has been sung through the ages with the words of David, the Psalmist. After each act of creation in Genesis 3 the refrain "And God saw that it was good" rings out in celebratory affirmation of the gift of life. Even the author of those occasionally strict and dour epistles in the New Testament speaks with the voice of a poet on the beauty of women's hair and the human form, divine as "the image and likeness" of God.

Yet in most Protestant traditions, and virtually all the communities that claim the Radical Reformation as their origin (including the Hutterian Brethren, Mennonites and Amish), beauty is safely tucked away and ritually proscribed. What Protestantism does in a general and average way, the Hutterian Brethren do with precision and spiritual discipline. Beauty is for God's eyes alone. To the fallen human nature, alas, its contemplation is a temptation, a temptation to be shunned.

The Hutterian Brethren understand themselves as a reform movement that reinstitutes the lifestyle of the early Christian communities. In 1528 a group of two hundred Anabaptists sought refuge from widespread persecution and established a communal society in Moravia under the leadership of Jakob Hutter. They restored the practice of communal living and the communal ownership of property based on the biblical teaching of "holding all things common." A critique of the sacramental theology of Roman Catholicism led to the Hutterites adopting Believer's Baptism. In this view, only adults, of their own free will and with full knowledge of the faith and a rejection of the worldly way of life, can enter fully into the church through baptism. Because the Bible teaches that God is the creator of all human beings—all are in the image and likeness of God—the Hutterites espouse an ethic of pacifism and are critical of all forms of war. They hold firmly to a separation of church (of which their colony is the proper example) and state.

The periodic persecutions of the Hutterian Brethren have caused numerous migrations. Throughout the more than 465 years of their communal life, they have sought refuge in Czechoslovakia, Hungary, Romania, tsarist Russia, the United States and Canada. Their refusal to participate in the Great War combined with their German culture and language led to considerable harassment and persecution in the United States. This provided the impetus for most of the world's Hutterites —sixty-six per cent of the twenty-five thousand Hutterites in the world—to migrate to western Canada. They still continue the most successful communal movement in modern history. In the Hutterite colonies of Canada, many of the original beliefs and customs and much of the dress, language and simple lifestyle have continued to flourish.

The disciplines of beauty are encountered by everyone who happens upon one of the many colonies of those who hold "all things common" or crosses the path of the "plain folk." Recognized in the cities and towns of western Canada by their dark and modest dress, Hutterite men, women and children appear to the public eye as members of a monastic community. Yet they marry, and it is in marriage that the vigorous shaping of the encounter with beauty can first be noted.

The sixteenth-century Brethren leader Ulrich Stadler, writing about the ordinance of procreation, said, "God, however, will wink at our marital work ... on behalf of children and will not reckon it upon those who act in fear and discipline." Beauty is not to be the object of human emotion or occasion of passion for anything other than the divine. Along with their singular regard for the sanctity of the human person—of which their pacifism is perhaps the most apt expression—the theological and spiritual tradition of the Brethren calls for all human relationships to be dispassionate.

In the early history of the movement, wives were called "marital sister" (*eheliche Schwester*) by their husbands. This sensibility was shaped in the early life of the community through a strict prohibition on courtship. Young men, the Polish nobleman Andreas Rey de Naglovitz reported from his visit to the colonies in Moravia in 1612, had the choice of three girls. The one chosen was "the will of God, whether young or old, poor or rich" (Peter Riedemann, *Rechenschaft unseres Glaubens*, 1540).

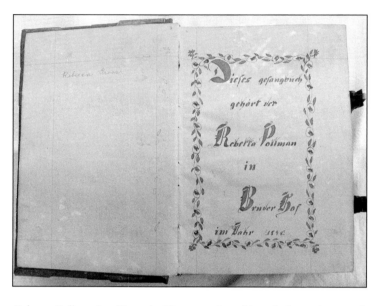

Rebecca Pollman's calligraphy illustrates the rubicated, decorative motifs used to embellish handwritten booklets in the Hutterian Brethren communities. This booklet, dated 1898, is in the Folklife Collection of the Provincial Museum of Alberta.

The regulations on matching couples for marriage changed modestly in the nineteenth century when the colonies' patron in the Molotschna district of Ukraine, Johann Cornies, intervened and established the opportunity for young people to make their own choice of life partner. The choices, of course, still had to be approved by the parents and colony elders before the announcement of an engagement. Marriage followed quickly, with perhaps three days elapsing before the Sunday wedding and the setting up of a new household. Of course, no one was fit for marriage who had not personally claimed Jesus Christ as the Saviour, the disciplines of the church as the guide and the community as the greatest asset in the growth in sanctity. All three were confirmed in the primary ordinance of initiation, Believer's Baptism.

Hutterian women prepare for marriage from early childhood. They are given a trunk in which to gather the necessities for the making of a home. The trunk typically occupies a place of importance in the family bedroom. Over the years its function grows, from the place where the gifts of cloth and yarn are stored before being made into clothing for the family, into an island of privacy. Part of the colony's gift to the young woman is cloth, needles, thread and other textile tools. The cloth is destined to be made by her into the clothing, sheets, towels and other household materials necessary for the new family. The rich community context and the benefits of extended family, however, make these tasks common ones. The women of the colony gather together on the long winter evenings to sew, knit, embroider and chat. Conviviality is part of the rhythm of everyday life.

It is not uncommon for the women of the colony to make friends in the various towns where they sell eggs and, after a time, to receive personal gifts from them. It may be a bottle of perfume, nylon stockings, jewellery or a photograph taken of them with their new friends. All these, of course, are prohibited within the public life of the colony and are discreetly tucked away in the trunk. Alongside these private treasures lie family heirlooms such as the clothing grandmothers made during the sojourn in Ukraine and the samplers made in childhood.

Bits and pieces of colourful cloth, buttons and ribbon are occasional acquisitions. These are also carefully tucked away, with only the slightest possibility that some of them will be put to use. And where are they used? If you examine the lining of clothing made on the colony, the unseen parts of garments, a world of colour opens up. Here the women, old and young alike, use the hidden garment—for no man will ever see—to let their eye for colour and loveliness flourish. The lining of "plain clothes" and undergarments becomes the landscape for colour, for the play of the imagination.

Another area of Hutterian folk art is in the diligent teaching of girls to use needle and thread to write their first letters and numbers, their first verses, homely bits of folk wisdom and biblical texts. These exercises are done from a very early age as samplers. Hutterite women characteristically save samplers from their early childhood along with some made by their mother and grandmother. The samplers are both generations of pedagogy and panels of loveliness and colour.

There is a common use for such panels beyond the teaching of lettering, numbering and the making of a fine stitch. Mirrors in the living quarters of colonies are often covered, since beauty is for God's eyes only. Samplers, the product of young hands, may be placed over the mirrors. A touch of beauty shields one from the temptations of vanity aroused by glimpsing the image and likeness of God in the mirror.

Beauty is for the eyes of God alone. Perhaps nowhere in the life of the Hutterian Brethren is this leitmotif so vividly present as in the act of the scribe. Within the Jewish tradition scribes continue to copy the *sefer Torah* for use in synagogues. This is done with great care and according to prescribed ritual and as an act of devotion. The only Christian tradition that still uses the scribe's role is the Hutterian Brethren. Here, however, the scribe is most often a woman and the text is from one of the many small sermon booklets (there are approximately six hundred) written before 1665.

When a colony grows to 150 souls (as the baptized are referred to), it is the custom to divide the colony in half and have one portion establish a new colony. Customarily, the mother colony purchases the land, machinery and building materials for its daughter colony. The first act in establishing the new colony is the election of a preacher, the keystone of the new community. He requires a set of the canon of sermons used in Hutterite worship services. The task of scribing these sermons often falls to a sister of the newly elected preacher.

In one case, the newly elected preacher purchased the paper for the work and his sister acquired the pen, nibs and ink. Since the materials are purchased with personal funds, the sister was mildly (perhaps playfully) annoyed about having to make some of the purchases. The paper is folded into signatures, gathered and sewn into a codex. The first letter beginning each major section of the sermon is rubricated, decorative motifs embellish the various pages and the title page is done with colour, grand lettering and a flair known only here in the public expression of Hutterian folk art.

Preachers prize these booklets and commission additional ones as well as collect older copies. This was not always so. The existence of a large number of written sermons of Hutterite origin was unknown in the scholarly literature until the publication in 1947 of the *Klein-Geschichtbuch der Hutterischen Brüder*, which included twenty-six sermons. All of these date from 1652 to 1659, the golden period of Hutterite spirituality. Most originated at a *Brüderhof* at Kesselsdorf in Slovakia, where a seminary seems to have flourished briefly. This material surfaced about 1800 as a result of the work of Johannes Waldner, a Hutterite bishop in Vishenka, Ukraine, who prepared a chronicle of Hutterite history from the sixteenth century through to his era. The chronicle was based on the sixteenth-century *Das große Geschichtbuch der Hutterischen Brüder*, known as the "big Chronicle."[1]

The careful collecting of the sermon booklets was begun in the eighteenth century as a result of the revival of the tradition of reading sermons during the worship service. The scribing of sermons was reinstituted, and Hutterites began working with the available examples. The earliest known sermon codex dates from 1786; additional copies dating to 1804 are known. Virtually all of these were taken to North America during the migration.

Each colony today has a collection of thirty to sixty carefully handwritten and bound copies of sermons for all occasions in the church year, including the holidays of Christmas, New Year's Day, Epiphany, Palm Sunday (the usual day for baptisms), Good Friday, Easter, Easter Monday and Tuesday, Ascension Day and Pentecost, with additional sermons for marriages, elections of ministers, funerals and other occasions. They are written and read in High German, which has become a kind of sacred language among the Hutterites, who speak a type of Tyrolean-Bavarian German dialect in everyday life.

The sermons are of two types, the *Lehren* and the *Vorreden*. Both are exegetical in character, with a *Lehre* focusing on a chapter of scripture with a lengthy (two hours is not uncommon) exposition and a *Vorrede* simply taking a verse and treating it in a short form. The preacher delivers the sermon in a chant. Hutterite preaching is referred to as sharp preaching, suggesting the radical nature of the demands of scripture on the faithful.

The scribing of new sermon booklets involves a number of people in proofreading. Each sermon is proofread by two other members—usually women—of the colony. An additional two members are called in to proofread all the quotations from scripture that are sprinkled throughout the sermons. This leads to long evenings reading and discussing the meaning of scripture to the life of the "remnant of God's people." It is out of this sensibility that I think the convention of always scribing the sermons comes. Hutterites have printed books for centuries, but the custom is that the canon of sermons is always to be handwritten.[2] This tradition assures that, periodically, a number of the brethren will take time to think about the meaning of the Gospel to their lives.

The challenge of recognizing beauty in the things of creation, of shaping its place within the life of the family and colony with attention to ritual proscription, falls largely to women. It is the women who are the keepers of the trunk in which cloth and thread, the means for adorning the body, are kept, and in which those little gifts that speak of friendship and another world and personal beauty are hidden away. It is the young girls, not yet fully initiated members of the community, who work with colour and form, perfecting their ability to make lovely letters, numbers and decorative motifs on samplers. Finally, it is the sister of each newly elected preacher who perfects her calligraphy, rubricates the opening letter of the sermons from the seventeenth century and decorates the borders of these pages that interpret the word of God. Beauty is for God's eyes only, and it falls to the women of the colony to walk the fine, ritually proscribed line as guardians of that beauty.

ACKNOWLEDGEMENT: When you learn something important from a man on the Hutterite colony it is referred to with the fond phrase, "receiving instruction." The author gratefully acknowledges the instruction he has received from Paul Gross of the Athabasca Hutterian Brethren Colony in Alberta and the many enjoyable conversations with Paul's sisters Mary and Rebecca. Through these conversations, the author's understanding of the spiritual perspectives of the Brethren was deepened.

NOTES

1. This foundational work on the formative years of the Hutterian Brethren is now available in English under the title *The Chronicle of the Hutterian Brethren*, translated and edited by the Hutterian Brethren (Rifton, New York: Plough Publishing House, 1987).

2. Some years ago, a member of a Canadian Hutterite colony learned about photocopying. He began to provide photocopies of these sermon booklets, arguing that the text was still written by hand.

APPROACHES TO WORD AND IMAGE IN GERMAN-CANADIAN FOLK ART

ROBERT B. KLYMASZ

Literacy influences almost all levels of human artistic expression in our society. Folk art, however, provides a middle ground, where the interplay of the written word and pictorial image allows a comparatively clear impression of the artist's intent. This interplay of word and image also makes folk art different from other kinds of artistic production.

The artistic traditions of Canada's German communities are especially rich in word-and-image forms, thanks to a legacy that is highly attuned to the needs and cultural requirements of a pervasive literacy. Fraktur and related forms of ornamental writing provide important insights into the nature of the German tradition. Many non-Germanic ethnocultural traditions in Canada avoid chirographic elements (writing or calligraphy) in their art, thereby highlighting the distinctiveness of German-Canadian folk art.[1]

The collections of the Canadian Centre for Folk Culture Studies at the Canadian Museum of Civilization contain two categories of word-plus-image artifacts: painting and needlework. Gender considerations affect any study of these artifacts, for male artists dominate as painters, and females outnumber males in producing art with needle and thread.

The paintings of Henry Pauls, a Mennonite Canadian, belong in the first category. His works have a strong narrative bent and are marked by moralistic overtones. For Pauls, biblical teachings are paramount; these teachings appear in chirographic forms ranging from brief aphorisms ("He who plants a garden, works hand in hand with God") and prayerful excerpts ("Give us this day our daily bread") to lengthier passages, such as the following verse, "Kneeling in a Garden":

This assembly of artwork by Henry Pauls shows Kneeling in a Garden *as the centrepiece of a larger configuration.*

There's a lot you can do in a garden
Besides raising onions and peas
It's the place where I know
All alone I can go
To set my distraught mind at ease.
There I dig down to true understanding
Resentments I weed at each bed.
And with rake and a hoe
While I'm kneeling I sow
New seeds of forgiveness instead.

There's so much you can do in a Garden
Besides pulling harmful weeds.
On your knees working there
You may think of a prayer
To offer for somebody's needs.
You can bury your heartaches and anger
Deep under the toughest of sod;
And you'll sweat as you hoe
But you'll certainly grow
In closer communion with God.

There's a lot you can do in a garden
Besides getting healthfully tired
As you hoe row on row
Watching everything grow,
With kindlier thoughts you're inspired.
Like a chapel for deep meditation
On weakness and personal strife,
In the garden you feel
As you labor and kneel
Impelled to make more out of life![2]

The rural content that is typical of Pauls' work is not confined to words alone. However, when text is used it always takes precedence. The text is often superimposed over inspirational, calming images of hope and faith such as the setting or rising sun, or village or farm landscapes. For contrast, it is useful to note the strikingly different way word-and-image configurations appear in the works of many contemporary Aboriginal Canadian artists. Like Pauls, many use English as the vehicle for verbal expression but exploit text and chirography in the commercial manner of billboards to convey powerful messages of rage and dismay.

English is also the language of choice in Hutterite presentation handkerchiefs, which form an intriguing part of the Centre's textile collections. Unlike paintings, samplers and Fraktur, the Hutterite handkerchief is not meant for public display; it is a personal statement with only one specific viewer in mind. An instrument of courtship and folk custom, the presentation handkerchief (for illustrations, see the section "From the Collections" in this volume) provides tangible evidence of a maiden's romantic interest in an eligible male of the community. It is addressed, signed and dated, and cites both giver and receiver by name. When folded and stuffed away in a pocket, the concealed handkerchief becomes a portable talisman burning with love-motifs: embroidered hearts, bells, flowers and vines. The handkerchief avoids the regimentation of Fraktur and related forms and focuses on intimacy by experimenting with words and images to suit the whims and talents of its maker. Its secretive message of affection and commitment does not follow the usual linear pattern of the printed line; rather, the words and motifs seem to be scattered in a way that anticipates the folds of the tucked-away handkerchief. When the handkerchief is pulled out, each unfolding reveals a new affirmation of devotion. The result is an accumulation of words and images that underline the handkerchief's intent and purpose.

NOTES

1. The East European folk tradition in Canada, for example, is underdeveloped in comparison with the productivity of Germanic chirography in Canada. For instance, anonymity is typical of Ukrainian sacred embroideries.

2. The verse is unsigned and was probably copied by Pauls from another source. I am indebted to Wesley Mattie of the Canadian Museum of Civilization for allowing me to draw upon his dossier of interview materials with Henry Pauls, including the verse replicated here.

BIBLIOGRAPHY

Bird, Michael S. *Ontario Fraktur: A Pennsylvania-German Folk Tradition in Early Canada.* Toronto: M.F. Feheley Publishers Ltd., 1977.

Klymasz, Robert B. "Stitching for God." *The Beaver*, December 1986 – January 1987, 46.

McMaster, Gerald, and Lee-Ann Martin, eds. *Indigena: Contemporary Native Perspectives.* Hull: Canadian Museum of Civilization, 1992.

Ong, Walter J. *Rhetoric, Romance, and Technology: Studies in the Interaction of Expression and Culture.* Ithaca, New York: Cornell University Press, 1971.

Patterson, Nancy-Lou Gellermann. *Swiss-German and Dutch-German Mennonite Traditional Art in the Waterloo Region, Ontario.* CCFCS Mercury Series No. 27. Ottawa: National Museum of Man, 1979.

"LOOK WHAT THESE HANDS HAVE DONE!"
MEANING IN GERMAN-CANADIAN FOLK ART

NANCY-LOU PATTERSON

Decoration is defined in Webster's Collegiate Dictionary as "to add something so as to make more." But the Indo-European base-word *dek* means "to do what is suitable"; it leads not only to *decoratus* (decorate), but to *dignus* (worthy) and *docere* (teach). These meanings make explicit the functions of folk art: to conform to the expectations of the group about what is suitable; to make worthy the occasion, purpose or action for which the object is made; and to teach what those expectations, suitabilities, values, occasions or actions mean.

Thus, the decoration of a well-made object goes beyond a desire for beauty or an instinct for embellishment. In interpreting the artifacts of traditional communities, one must address the cognitive dimension, which is always operating along with the material dimension. The cognitive dimension includes both ethical and aesthetic elements; as Reinhild and John Janzen state, "There are no aesthetically neutral customs. Even those behaviours which are overtly technical have a dimension of symbolic responsiveness which reveals the ethics as well as the aesthetics of a community."

The cognitive dimension reaches beyond ethics and aesthetics to include the sacred, that is, an awareness of the world as filled with meaning and reality. In this context, activities such as gathering food, having children and making objects are sacramental. In the rural Mennonite communities of Waterloo County, for example, farming is a "sacred vocation," in the words of a senior Mennonite scholar, J. Winfield Fretz.

The very form of folk artifacts symbolizes an orderly universe. Form *is* meaning. The simplest looking structures, those incorporating binary sets, demonstrate this meaning. Folk art artifacts are nearly always symmetrical and bilateral. They illustrate the extremely archaic human understanding of orientation. Orientation is the perception of the world as a place where the human body—head above, feet below, hands to either side, face front and back behind—exactly reflects the structure of the cosmos.

The characteristic heraldic composition is a good example of this orderly universe. A central figure facing the viewer is flanked by two escorts who face each other. This composition goes well beyond formality to imply the importance of the central figure and the subsidiary roles of the flanking figures. When two figures stand side by side, on the other hand, they are being shown as related and equal. In the same way, compositions often place the superior figure above and the inferior figure below. Sometimes even the left and right positioning of figures is used to show their value.

All symmetrical figures are embodiments of order. The arrangement of elements in orderly ways—symmetry rather than asymmetry, balance rather than imbalance—implies not only a sense of order on the part of the artist but a celebration of balance, harmony and stability. The ornament that accompanies such formal structures and arrangements has similar intentions. Specific motifs are used for ornaments because they are commonly understood as seemly or appropriate.

Why *these* motifs in particular? Through the innovation of the printed book, sample-books of ornamental motifs spread across Europe from Germany in the early sixteenth century. Based on hand-drawn sample sheets used in the textile, metalwork and book trades, these sample-books included geometric and representational elements of the Islamic, Gothic and Renaissance traditions. The books detached ornament from object to make a range of motifs available across time and distance. They put the cultural heritage of the elite into the hands of the many, at the beginning of an era when the art of the incipient middle class was feeding a new and ever-expanding taste for personal possessions and objects of virtue.

German-Canadian folk art motifs echo European folk art motifs: geometric elements such as lozenges, hatching and crenellations; compass-drawn designs (like those published by Albrecht Dürer in 1525) such as six-pointed stars, whorls and lobed swastikas; and interlacement and knotwork motifs including the pentangle (five-pointed star), derived via Venice from the Near East. Representational motifs are many: Adam and Eve under the Tree of Paradise, and Joshua and Caleb with the grapes; cavaliers and ladies, like those in Johannes Sibmacher's *Neues Modelbuch* of 1604, accounting for a variety of mounted males (soldiers and hunters) as well as elegantly dressed female figures; the ubiquitous heart, especially common in the written forms of Switzerland, Austria, South Germany and Alsace, and hence in Canada; fabulous creatures such as mermaids; animals domestic (peacocks, roosters and horses) and undomestic (doves, pelicans and lions); plants, including the garland, the vessel of flowers, the rosette, the acanthus cluster and the flowering tree, all obviously derived from classical ornament perpetuated into the Renaissance; heraldic motifs, including the two-headed eagle, the lion and the unicorn. Finally, there are the scripts, both Gothic and Roman, used in mottoes, names, monograms and dates, forms of calligraphy perpetuated by books of printed samples.

German-Canadian works of folk art show all these categories of motif. Nova Scotia's Germanic folk art makes generous use of geometric elements, as well as floral and other classical forms; the lobed swastika is a distinguishing motif of this region. Southern Ontario, except for the swastika, offers a complete range of European folk art motifs, probably because of the great variety of German-speaking ethnic, religious and regional communities. Also used are the "ribbon star" (an eight-pointed star, often called the German star) and, a motif distinct to Renfrew County, a teardrop shape sometimes arranged to radiate like the flutes of a scallop shell. The Prairie provinces repeat a selection of the more abstract motifs but emphasize classical devices such as volutes, scrollwork, corner motifs and quasi-realistic flowers.

What do these elements mean? Briefly, abstract or geometric ornaments signify order, and representational elements signify life. Overtly religious motifs taken from the Bible are the most specific. The image of Adam and Eve with the Tree of Paradise, for example, celebrates creation, paradise, redemption, godliness and eternal life; the image of Joshua and Caleb with the grapes from Canaan symbolizes the promised land. Idealized landscapes and "home-place" paintings often echo these themes. Most specifically, the crucifix (often seen in both Lutheran and Roman Catholic Germanic works) presents the entire salvific message of Christianity in a single motif. Sometimes, overtly Christian images lose their specific meanings and forms. Examples are the transformation of the "pelican feeding her young from her own blood," a symbol of Christ, into the "birds in a nest" motif, in which baby birds wait alone without their mother; and the "table and chairs" motif, a symbol of hospitality based on depictions of the Lord's Table bearing a chalice and two ewers, later being reduced to a pitcher and two cups.

Such explicit or formerly explicit images are rare, however. Considerably more common are vegetal and floral motifs, anonymous even when identified as tulip, carnation or rose. According to Reinhild and John Janzen, flowers are "a universal symbol of validating significant events in the human life cycle." Like biblical motifs, flowers are used on dowry items, including textiles, to express the ethical dimensions of marriage and family; that is, that marriage and family are central to the structure and perpetuation of the community. Similarly, flowers are displayed on artifacts in the context of birth, baptism, betrothal, marriage and burial, as well as to express love, gratitude, personal achievement and the cycle of the church year.

The heart as a symbol of love appeared on a Christian lamp in Switzerland in the sixth century. In twelfth-century France the heart became associated with romance, and in late medieval and counter-Reformation settings it was used as a Christian symbol. In ancient art the heart also signified life, and this meaning, too, continues into the present. Animals and birds also carry the message of life and fecundity, and thus exuberantly occupy the flowered and treed environment of folk ornament. All these forms celebrate life and encourage love to follow the channels society has provided for its expression.

Geometric forms are equally abundant. Stars, whorls, swastikas, compass-drawn figures, crescents, the *Ur-bogen* (origin bow, which traces the arc of the rising and setting sun)—all these refer to celestial phenomena as symbols of cosmic order, just as they have done since ancient times. Like biblical motifs, they express wonder and delight in the creation.

The artist calls upon these cosmic witnesses (so often depicted in medieval scenes of the crucifixion) to lend their light to the purposes and occasions of the objects they adorn.

In the context of folk usage, ornaments placed upon artifacts signify value, and ornamented objects associated with life events signify propriety. Images and artifacts served the specific needs of the families by and for whom they were made; as Wilson Duff wrote, "The most important use of some of man's implements is to carry his symbols."

What is the role of the individual artist in all this collective activity, and by what symbol or sign is the individual made known? Writers on folk art often meditate on the relations of "individual creativity and collective order." Michael Bird has postulated a division of folk art into "idiosyncratic," which "is a form of personal expression," and "ethnosyncratic," which "has a collective orientation." Since the advent of printed pattern-books, folk artists of both stripes have experienced innovation through, and taken inspiration from, broadly disseminated mass media; both kinds of artist take personal pleasure in their work, and both find personal expression in what they make. Simon J. Bonner, writing of chain carvers, says, "The things individuals create which call on tradition can become symbolic autobiography, ... reliant as they are on a sense of self and connection with others."

The role of individuals as makers or owners is given expression in the written, painted or carven word, most significantly in the personal name, a much more common expression of individuality than the portrait. This category of folk ornament, developed in Europe, flourished in North America, notably in Fraktur but also in embroidered names and initials. Printed and handwritten items continued into the twentieth century, as did the marking of dowry items. Such documents bespeak a powerful sense of identity. Indeed, Pastor Frederick S. Weiser finds the origins of German-Canadian folk art "in the striving of the peasant and small craftsmen levels of society for a sense of identity in the Germanic lands of Central Europe from the end of the Thirty Years' War to the onset of industrialization." This tradition of identity expressed in personal names and lovingly made images and objects is continued in Canada today by the descendants of such artists.

The title of my essay comes from the words of a woman in her nineties, a Dutch-German Mennonite from Waterloo County. In January 1992, she was brought to see the exhibition "White on White" at the Joseph Schneider Haus Museum in Kitchener, Ontario. There she saw a display of exquisite whitework textiles that she had embroidered as a young girl in prerevolutionary South Russia, using patterns from a German pattern-book of that era. Holding out her gnarled fingers, she exclaimed to her daughter, "Look what these hands have done!" Her embroideries, so anonymous and collective, so characteristic of a group, a time, a style, were and are absolute validation of her own life, her own skill and her own identity. This, perhaps most of all, is the meaning of folk art.

BIBLIOGRAPHY

Bird, Michael, and Terry Kobayashi. *A Splendid Harvest: Germanic Folk and Decorative Arts in Canada*. Toronto: Van Nostrand Reinhold, 1981.

Bird, Michael. *Canadian Folk Art: Old Ways in a New Land*. Toronto: Oxford University Press, 1983.

Bonner, Simon J. *Chain Carvers: Old Men Crafting Meaning*. Lexington, Kentucky: The University Press of Kentucky, 1985.

Duff, Wilson. *Images, Stone, BC*. Toronto: Oxford University Press, 1975.

Eliade, Mircea. *A History of Religious Ideas*. Vol. 1. Chicago: University of Chicago Press, 1978.

Fretz, J. Winfield. *The Waterloo Mennonites: A Community in Paradox*. Waterloo: Wilfrid Laurier Press, 1989.

Glassie, Henry. *The Spirit of Folk Art*. New York: Harry N. Abrams, 1989.

Hersh, Tandy, and Charles Hersh. *Samplers of the Pennsylvania Germans*. Birdsboro, Pennsylvania: The Pennsylvania German Society, 1991.

Janzen, Reinhild K., and John M. Janzen. *Mennonite Furniture: A Migrant Tradition (1766–1910)*. Intercourse, Pennsylvania: Good Books, 1991.

Lee-Whiting, Brenda. *Harvest of Stones: The German Settlement in Renfrew County*. Toronto: University of Toronto Press, 1985.

Patterson, Nancy-Lou. "Gardens, Hearts, and Distelfinken; Mennonite Folk Art Symbols." *Canadian Collector*, September 1984, 36–39.

———. "The Iconography of the Show Towel," *Waterloo Historical Society 64* (1976): 49–67.

———. "Landscape and Meaning: Structure and Symbolism of the Swiss-German Mennonite Farmstead of Waterloo Region, Ontario." *Canadian Ethnic Studies* 16, 3(1984): 35–52.

———. The Language of Paradise. London, Ontario: The London Regional Art Gallery, 1985.

———. "Meditative Hearts: Heart Symbolism in Mennonite Folk Art of Southern Ontario." *Waterloo Historical Society* 70 (1983): 32–49.

———. *Swiss-German and Dutch-German Mennonite Traditional Art in the Waterloo Region, Ontario*. CCFCS Mercury Series No. 27. Ottawa: National Museums of Canada, 1979.

———. "The Sacred Vocation: Swiss-German Mennonite Landscape Concepts." In *Perspectives of Canadian Landscape: Minority Traditions*. Ed. Joan M. Vastokas. North York, Ontario: The Robarts Centre, York University, 1991.

———. "'See the Vernal Landscape Glowing': The Symbolic Landscape of the Swiss-German Mennonite Settlers in Waterloo County." *Mennonite Life,* December 1983, 8–16.

———. "Where One Teaches God's Word: Image and Text in Mennonite Folk Art." *Mennogespräch*, March 1990, 1–4, 7–8.

Peesch, Reinhard. *The Ornament in European Folk Art*. New York: Alpine Fine Arts Collection, 1983.

Weiser, Pastor Frederick S. "Foreword." In Bird, Michael, and Terry Kobayashi. *A Splendid Harvest: Germanic Folk and Decorative Arts in Canada*. Toronto: Van Nostrand Reinhold, 1981.

Diversity and Flux in Manitoba Mennonite Material Culture

Steve Prystupa

Canadian ethnic groups are still widely perceived as enclaves of traditional cultures that sooner or later are absorbed into the mainstream through assimilation or modernization. In western Canada, this perception applies especially to rural ethnic bloc settlements formed by groups such as the Mennonites, Hutterites, Ukrainians, Germans, Mormons and Doukhobours. In recent years, however, serious questions have been raised about the underlying folk-versus-modern stereotype. Were these groups really as traditional as generally proposed? Were they merely passive followers in the processes of commercialization, urbanization and modernization, or were they, in certain respects, key players? Is ethnicity somehow incompatible with these dimensions of contemporary culture? Does the popular present-day portrayal of ethnic groups through folk art, music, dance and food adequately articulate the uniqueness of each group? Historians and social scientists have contributed significantly in recent years to the reinterpretation of the issues raised here. Mennonite scholars have been especially assiduous in redefining the ground of ethnic inquiry, especially as it relates to their own group.

Cultural Dynamics

The historical evolution of the Mennonites reflects a dynamic relationship between their Anabaptist core values, changing historical circumstances, encounters with other cultures and the need to adapt to new economic trends and geographic settings. As Leo Driedger has shown, the core values provide a thread of continuity from past to present.

Adult baptism and pacifism are beliefs shared today by practically all Mennonite communities, from the most conservative rural Mennonites to the most liberal suburban churches. In other respects, the differences between the Mennonite churches are as great as the differences between other Protestant denominations. This broad range of options, which Driedger calls the "Anabaptist ladder," enables individual Mennonites to move up and down the ladder from the most orthodox to the most progressive levels without leaving the Mennonite fold.

Even the conservative communities cannot really be defined as traditional. Historically, defiance of established authority, repeated migrations and the need to adapt to new environments have produced a culture that emphasizes process and principle rather than place and tradition. Scholars have characterized the Mennonites as intentional or ideological communities to distinguish them from the traditional place-oriented understanding of a community. In certain respects, they are an Anabaptist equivalent of the wandering Jew—universally adaptable and yet never quite at home. Change is an integral part of both cultures. During each successive stage of Mennonite history—in the Netherlands, in Prussia, in Ukraine and in Canada—momentous changes occurred. When necessary, the Mennonites migrated, either for rededication to the faith or as a strategy of survival. In effect, they created a mobile culture, which, like a ship at sea, adjusts its sails and takes a new tack when the prevailing winds change.

With the strong emphasis that Mennonites place on religious principles and practice, one might expect a rich assemblage of religious objects within their material culture. In fact, the boundary between sacred and secular has been blurred ever since the Anabaptist movement began in the sixteenth century. The Mennonite desire to retreat from worldly temptations within a fellowship of believers, as well as their periodic need to be unobtrusive in order to escape persecution, led to an unassuming—some might say lacklustre—religious aesthetic, secular in its outward appearance. Buildings, furnishings, clothing and other objects used in Mennonite worship still tend to reflect this ideal. Some objects may be discreetly decorated or finely designed, but on the whole there is little gleam or glitter.

The religious material culture is used by the Mennonites to define themselves as a people apart. Their everyday life is deeply permeated by the same ascetic ideals. Because of their plain clothes and simple, if not austere, way of life, early Mennonites were called "plain" or "peculiar" people. These terms were used by outsiders but were also self-ascribed.

Historically, the Mennonites have also taken a strong position against religious hierarchies. They believe that preachers and other church officers should be elected from the laity, should work for their livelihood and should not use special religious garb or other symbols of authority. Hence, mitres, staffs, rings and clerical vestments are nonexistent. This democratic Anabaptist organizational structure at both the congregation and conference level precludes a show of rank and status.

The emphasis on plainness extends into actual religious observances. Highly symbolic rituals such as the celebration of the mass were abandoned in the sixteenth century in favour of evangelical forms of worship—Bible study, hymn singing and the reading of sermons. There are no ornate communion vessels, censers, icons, candlesticks or holy-water founts for the administration of rites such as communion, baptism, marriage and burial. Instead, unadorned utensils are used, and special forms such as baptism by immersion are practised within some congregations.

Of late, occasional banners, stained glass and spires have become common, but some communities still prefer the simple prayer-house structure instead of more explicit church architecture and decor. The use of classical sacred music and instruments such as the organ, piano and guitar is uncharacteristic of conservative rural congregations but is optional in more liberal urban congregations. On the whole, such changes do not detract from the essentially ascetic quality and simplicity of religious life.

The flux and diversity that characterize Mennonite religious life are parallelled by diverse ethnic influences. Today, most social scientists and historians regard the Mennonites interchangeably as an ethnic and a religious group. Mennonites themselves have mixed feelings about this nomenclature. Some do not wish to compromise their religious mission as a Christian fellowship with ethnic adjectives. (Mennonite doctrine advocates adult baptism—that is, membership by conscious choice and commitment—and opposes membership that is determined by ancestry alone.) Others oppose the ethnic designation because, increasingly, people from other ethnic groups and races are joining the Mennonite church. There are also individuals of Mennonite ancestry who do not choose to belong to the church or who, in earlier days especially, were excommunicated. These are complicating factors within the community, but they cannot negate the original ethnic antecedents of the group and the diverse ethnic influences that have shaped it since then.

Western Canadian Mennonites hail almost exclusively from the Dutch provinces of Friesland and Flanders and the adjacent north German districts. They take their name from a Dutch Mennonite leader, Menno Simons. Internal persecution by the established Catholic and state churches forced these dissidents from the radical wing of the Reformation to migrate to Prussia. For a century, the Dutch refugees maintained the Dutch language in these north German settlements, but by 1750 the German language had been adopted in their schools. High German became the language of literature and formal religious practice. The Low German dialect of the Vistula Delta area, known as *Plautdietsch*, became the Mennonites' vernacular language. In this way, a tier of German culture was grafted onto their principally Dutch background and remains a central feature of Mennonite ethnicity.

In the late eighteenth and early nineteenth century, the Mennonites lost some of their settlement privileges in Prussia and migrated to southern Ukraine. The occupation of the Dnieper valley area began in 1789 and the settlement of the Molotschna area in 1803. Eventually, daughter colonies extended into Russia and Siberia. The Mennonites transplanted their Dutch Anabaptist beliefs and elements of German culture into Eastern Europe. However, those who came to Manitoba in 1874–77 reflected almost a century of Ukrainian and Russian influences, which affected their material culture in myriad ways. Those who arrived in the 1920s and 1940s had experienced even greater Russifying influences and were referred to as *Russlanders* (distinguishing them from the original Mennonite settlers, known as *Kanadier*). The *Kanadier*, despite their conservative orientation, had already learned the English language and adopted certain Canadian practices, or helped to shape them.

In the 1920s, Manitoba Mennonite colonies were created in Mexico. Colonies were subsequently established in Belize, Paraguay and Bolivia; these colonies included conservative groups from previous settlements as well as new refugees from the Soviet Union. Many of these still engage in a migratory drift back and forth between Canada and Latin America. The result has been new infusions of conservative influences and *Plautdietsch* as well as certain Latin ethnic influences.

The proliferation of Mennonite colonies throughout the western hemisphere was parallelled by mounting Mennonite missionary efforts in Asia and Africa as well as Latin America. Here in Canada, Aboriginal Canadians and other minorities were persuaded to adopt the Mennonite faith.

These numerous points of contact with diverse peoples of the world have given Mennonite ethnicity and religion a cosmopolitan cast. This quality militates against earlier religious aloofness and subtly affects the original Dutch and German folkways and material culture. The ethnic consciousness of the group is once again in flux, as numerous Mennonite scholars have pointed out in recent studies. Manitoba Mennonites from the original immigrant stock view these accretions and transformations with a mixture of excitement, pride and anxiety.

ECONOMIC UNDERPINNINGS

There is a certain risk in drawing a close connection between material and nonmaterial culture. Mennonite core values persist despite over four centuries of profound economic changes. Yet it is true that the radical reformation spearheaded by the Anabaptists and the persecutions that they endured had as much to do with their place in the early capitalist economic order as with their opposition to the institutional churches. Moreover, their insistence on desacralizing religion and leading a simple, ascetic life fostered frugality and industriousness. With their migration to Prussia at the end of the sixteenth century, they achieved a modicum of economic stability. This enabled them to establish a niche as master craftsmen and farmers (*Bauernvolk*). The substantial domestic architecture and furniture that they created during this period signified participation in a commercial economy. Some even entered business and industry.

When they moved to southern Ukraine in the mid-eighteenth century, they carried their material culture and economic skills with them. This was a new frontier of capitalist economic expansion, an early phase of the great nineteenth- and twentieth-century expansion of commercial agriculture into the temperate grasslands of the world. Settling on the steppes of Ukraine and Russia (and later in North America), the Mennonites were in the vanguard of this process. They chose locations along rivers and close to Black Sea ports, thus gaining easy access to the European wheat market. An Agricultural Commission and model farm were established by the 1830s to promote the latest scientific and commercial farming methods. By mid-century, major farm implement factories and flour mills were established. These industries and the cash economy led to the growth of Mennonite towns and the emergence of Mennonite suburbs in some larger Slavic cities. The attainment of this level of economic development challenges the notion that the Mennonites transplanted traditional peasant culture in Manitoba.

In their classic work on North American ethnic settlement patterns, Hansen and Brebner underline the importance of the so-called *Aufmarschgebiet*, the staging area in an earlier settlement from which new frontiersmen are drawn as settlement advances. Mennonite migration history provided a succession of such staging areas, and they became ideal frontiersmen. The notion of a good frontiersman is often taken to mean a person on the make, a risk-taker—especially a single man. Actually, the long-term success of new settlements has always been facilitated by the ability to relocate whole families and communities from one frontier to the next. This process of serial settlement can be traced by the recurrence of certain place names.

The Mennonites provide an ideal example of this settlement process. Place names like Blumengart, Reinfeld, Rosenthal and Sommerfeld can be traced from original sites in Ukraine and Prussia to Manitoba and thence to Saskatchewan, Alberta and Latin America. The Mennonite house-barn compound, the concentration of settlers in an agricultural village and strong kinship networks provided a broad-based adaptive system for the occupation of new frontiers. Moreover, even the poorer Old Colony Mennonites who arrived in Manitoba in the 1870s brought assets averaging $969 per settler. It was a substantial sum for that period and, as Royden Loewen has shown, the Mennonites quickly developed a commercial economy here. The population grew from six thousand in 1877 to eighteen thousand by the end of the First World War.

Ingenious as the agricultural village was for pioneering, it began to give way to the Canadian system of individual farmsteads within a generation. When six thousand of the most conservative Mennonites left Manitoba for Mexico in the 1920s, they were replaced by eight thousand new arrivals. These were more well-to-do, liberal-thinking Mennonites who had chosen to remain in Eastern Europe in the 1870s but were now impelled to move by the Bolshevik revolution. This changeover hastened the abandonment of the farm-occupied villages and consolidated the family farm.

By exploiting the Winnipeg market for meat, poultry and dairy products, developing special crops such as sugar beets, sunflower and corn and relying on family labour, the Mennonites were able to support twice as many people per unit area as adjacent non-Mennonite farmers. Instead of trying to maintain their separate schools and municipal government, they were able to take control of the public institutions in their area. Ecological concentration facilitated community cohesiveness.

Urban trades, occupations and industries have been traced to the original communities in the Netherlands and Prussia. Community schools developed both language and mathematical literacy. This is evident in the abundance of old letters, account books and narratives. The notion of measured time was also acquired very early. The so-called Mennonite clock, evolved from an earlier Dutch version, was manufactured in Prussia by the end of the eighteenth century, and Mennonite clockmakers continued to produce them in Ukraine. Such small craftsmen went on to develop major machine industries. The first grain-harvesting combine in the Soviet Union was produced in a Mennonite plant in the 1920s.

Thus, urbanization and modernization were well advanced in the Old Country at the time the Mennonites were taking up land in Manitoba. The growth of Mennonite towns in this province began with the location of stores and flour mills in enterprising farm villages like Altona and Steinbach and the gravitation of Mennonite businesses to nearby commercial towns like Winkler and Gretna. In time, the Mennonites became the dominant element in virtually all the rural towns within their settlement area. Larger regional towns like Steinbach, Winkler and Altona became prominent in food processing industries, retail sales and small manufacturing.

The first Mennonite families settled in Winnipeg around 1907, but significant growth did not begin until the 1920s when the wave of *Russlander* refugees arrived. These, together with a further influx of Second World War refugees, formed the core of the Winnipeg community. By the 1960s there was a trickle of migrants from colonies in Mexico and Paraguay. Between 1940 and 1980, large-scale rural–urban migration began, creating economic, congregational and kinship networks between rural Mennonites and the city. Today, almost half of Manitoba's sixty-five thousand Mennonites reside in Winnipeg. They are served by forty-six churches, which represent virtually every subgroup on the Anabaptist ladder.

Urban Mennonites can be found in practically every trade and profession. However, there is an interesting continuity with the historic Mennonite craft tradition and industrial development in Europe. Furniture making, machine industries and building trades predominate. According to Leo Driedger's estimates, Mennonite businesses and industries employ ten thousand workers. In Winnipeg and rural towns, the Mennonite homes are indistinguishable from others except for occasional glimpses of nostalgic titbits from the past, such as lace curtains, rows of geraniums and Dutch windmill lawn ornaments. The churches continue to be unobtrusive structures, which in their own modest way declare a continuing commitment to plainness in worship.

The historic emphasis of Mennonites on looking after their own was reflected in a village organization called the *Waisenamt*; it provided a form of social insurance to members. The German school was an integral part of every village. Today there is a rapidly growing complex of urban Mennonite institutions including social-service agencies, retirement homes, hospitals, Bible colleges, Christian publishing houses, disaster-relief organizations and world missions. Mennonite names on business establishments also declare the Mennonite presence. Original Dutch or German names such as Reimer, Penner, Ens, Neufeld, Toews, Loewen, Friesen and Klassen predominate, rivalling the Joneses and Smiths in southern Manitoba telephone books.

ARTICULATING MENNONITE

PRINT CULTURE. The roots of Anabaptism can be directly linked to the invention of the printing press, which made the printed word broadly accessible to ordinary people. Mennonite archives, museums and even private homes in Manitoba contain early Dutch and German copies of religious chronicles, tracts on doctrinal subjects such as adult baptism and passive resistance to war, confessions of faith, hymn-books and collections of sermons. Of the greatest significance were the personal works of early church leaders like Menno Simons, Conrad Grebel and Dirk Phillips and martyrological accounts such as Van Braght's *Martyrs Mirror*, compiled in 1660. These provide a historic creation myth focusing on Mennonite ethnogenesis and baptism by fire. This myth was subsequently reinforced by Mennonite experiences during the Bolshevik revolution and the two world wars.

Ever since the sixteenth century, Mennonite discourse has been abundantly provided with inspirational writers, argumentative doctrinal tracts and biographies, which personalize church teachings and aid worship. The first writings were Dutch, but by 1750 High German had been adopted. Today, many Mennonites still read German, but English has become the language of common parlance. Numerous translations have been produced to meet this need.

Arnold Dyck began to write Low German comic stories in the 1930s, and since the 1960s a growing repertoire of Canadian Mennonite fiction has appeared. It includes such prominent English-language writers as Rudy Wiebe and Patrick Friesen. Recent anthologies of English-language writing in the journal *Prairie Fire* and the book *Unter dem Nordlicht* show a continuing interest in historic and religious themes, rural nostalgia and Low German idiom. As Maurice Mierau observes in *Prairie Fire* (Vol. 11, No. 2, 1990), "Our ancestors were funny people, they wanted to tell the truth all the time."

The first Mennonite print shop was established in Ukraine in 1887. Historical writings were greatly stimulated by the 1889 centennial of the migration to Ukraine. By 1900, fiction, drama, children's stories, devotional works, biographies, calendar almanacs, newspapers and magazines were being published. American Mennonite publications were also available. Thus, early Manitoba Mennonites were part of a print culture from the outset. A print shop set up in Steinbach in 1901 eventually became Derksen Printers. D.W. Friesen Printers of Altona was in business by the 1930s, and several magazines and newspapers were locally published. After the Second World War, the Christian press became more and more prominent.

SINGING MENNONITE. Hymn singing was an integral part of Mennonite worship in the Netherlands, but the Dutch influence waned when the German language was adopted in the 1750s. The use of High German as a language of worship ultimately opened the Mennonites to influences from the immense German sacred and classical music repertoire. At first, however, the influence was primarily from Lutheran and other Reformed Church hymnals. The initial absence of notated hymnals in Ukraine led to subtle changes in melodies, which were later perpetuated by conservative Canadian congregations. According to Winnipeg choir director Georg Wiebe, these hymns were characterized by a penetrating nasal tone and a slow tempo, necessary to accommodate the many ornamental notes that had been added.

A German *Gesangbuch* published in 1837 tried to retrieve the original German forms. Numerical notations (*Ziffern*) were used instead of staff notations. These reduced the complexity of the tunes for amateurs and enabled sophisticated choir directors to recreate classical subtleties, but they were not suitable for instrumental music. The formation of the Mennonite Brethren Church in 1860 and its adoption of the Baptist hymnal opened the door to more joyous forms of hymn singing, although some congregations were careful not to be too joyous.

Initially, only school choirs existed, but gradually village choirs took over and choral festivals were organized. A few instrumental groups also emerged in progressive communities. The village of Chortitza even had a brass band. Some of these innovations were carried over to Manitoba with the arrival of the *Russlanders*. Eventually, classical sacred music was enthusiastically adopted. Mennonite performers and conductors also became highly accomplished in nonreligious choral and orchestral music. Their influence has been felt in public-school choirs, at music festivals and on the professional stage as well as in their own congregations and schools.

There are mixed feelings about this growing sophistication in Mennonite music. One reviewer for example, asks, "How much real cultural gain do we make by replacing the naive but honest 'Schlichtheit' of our forefathers with the sophisticated facade of the main culture? Do we gain or lose by translating their rugged simplicity into a slick contemporary idiom?" Others, like musicologist Doreen Klassen and the Low German performing group *Heischraitje en Willa Honich*, have deliberately tried to collect extant Low German secular songs and popularize them on the public stage. As Klassen indicates, some of their original simplicity is lost, but they do contribute to a sense of Mennonite peoplehood.

The ethnic music culture has been facilitated by the gradual removal of conservative restrictions on jug-band instruments, which are part of the folk tradition. However, in the last analysis, contemporary Mennonite popular culture favours Christian music most of all, if one can judge by the number of discs and tapes that are produced. A new multiethnic sensibility is reflected in the multilingual *International Songbook* that was released for the 1976 World Congress and in the interjection of dance into religious observances at gatherings such as the World Congress by non-European Mennonites.

CULTURAL LANDSCAPE. The Mennonite house-barn structure that characterized all Mennonite villages in Canada for the first generation or two can be directly traced to the Dutch longhouse. It was so designated because it was normally positioned parallel rather than perpendicular to the canal, stream or street, and the attachment of a barn at one end made it appear even longer. This building design was carried over more or less intact to East Prussia, where local influences resulted in the addition of a massive central chimney and bake oven, which served as a central heating system for the kitchen, living room and bedrooms surrounding it. In Ukraine, this architectural form was placed within the framework of a street village, which ideally would be laid out along a stream. Each farm family had its own garden plot in the back, and larger strip fields for cultivating crops outside the village. This unique settlement matrix was an important physical expression of a people apart.

With urbanization and the professionalization of culture, a growing number of Mennonite architects and builders now combine traditional building types and contemporary structures. They are aware of historic forms, and their work shows the continuing influence of plainness and frugality, especially in churches and institutional buildings. Recently, for example, in the design of a new Mennonite restaurant in Winnipeg, the Mennonite architect Harold Funk tried to re-create the layout and feeling of a traditional Mennonite house-barn compound. The restaurant includes a central fireplace and some of the woodworking features. The new Mennonite Heritage Centre and Archives, Winnipeg, was also designed by a Mennonite architect. The high-pitched roof incorporated into the pleasing pyramid-like structure is reminiscent of the house-barn profile. The inside creates an intimate and respectful atmosphere for the community's most treasured historical and religious documents and books.

Outside of examples like these, it is difficult to pinpoint specific Mennonite elements within present-day Canadian design and use of materials. Mennonite builders, of whom there are many, are integral to Canada's building industry. Martin Bergen, a prominent Winnipeg apartment developer and builder, is an interesting example. Arriving as a tradesman after the Second World War, he became adept at using new materials such as precast concrete and identifying new needs such as seniors' towers. More recently he has turned to the luxury market, with ostentatious structures like his "Castle on the Seine" and a postmodern apartment tower, which features replicas of classical sculpture and a twelfth-floor revolving restaurant. These diverse buildings are contemporary reflections of the continuing tension between Mennonite ideals, business enterprise and economic success.

ZWIEBACH AND VARENIKI. In the everyday life of ethnic groups, food is often the strongest indicator of ethnic persistence and reflects dominant cultural influences. Mennonite food reflects two principal aspects of the group's background—its agricultural roots and its ethnic diversity. Meat was not very important in the original Dutch menu, but vegetables, dairy products such as cheese and baking specialties like peppernut cookies, pancakes, waffles and apple fritters were common. The use of honey, currants and raisins with bread and cereals was also characteristic. Certain meats and cabbage were combined with prunes and raisins.

In Prussia, vegetables diminished in importance but ham, pork chops, pork roast and sausages came into common use. Zwiebach, originally a baked and reheated bun, became a Mennonite specialty. In Ukraine, borsch and vareniki became staples and seasonal items like paska were added. Watermelons were widely grown and, as Norma Voth writes, became a Russian-Mennonite addiction. They were eaten fresh, used as prepared fruits and even used to make drinks. Canadian Mennonite cookbooks, now popular, contain recipes from all these backgrounds as well as various new recipes appropriated from other Canadians. Families who have continuing contacts with Latin America also prepare foods reflecting a Latin influence.

Mennonite businessmen have capitalized on this culinary tradition. Usually starting as corner-store operations, a number of Mennonite food stores have become large, intercity, supermarket operations. A symbiotic relationship is maintained with local farmers and food processors in rural Mennonite areas. Such economic ties reinforce kinship networks. These shops also generally stock a wide selection of imported Dutch and German cheeses, breads, biscuits, preserves and chocolates. Mennonite bakeries are common in Mennonite rural towns and urban neighbourhoods; Dutch bakers also gravitate to such areas. With urbanization, Mennonite restaurants have become quite numerous. Some, like the *d'8 Shtove* in Winnipeg, list menu items in Low German. Items like *Rhepspaih, Glomms Kuuk, Wrenikji* and *Schinke Fleesh*, as well as distinctive Mennonite farmer's sausage, may appear exotic or mysterious to outsiders. For Mennonites, they evoke strong nostalgic feelings and help to define who they are. Traditional foods are a strong element of continuity in a constantly changing culture, and enrich and reinforce extended family ties.

INSIDER AS OUTSIDER. Rembrandt and other Dutch painters of the sixteenth and seventeenth centuries had Mennonite connections. They produced works of a secular nature as well as on biblical subjects. After the Dutch period, the biblical injunction against graven images held sway. Although not always restricting decorative art or art for its own sake, the churches did not generally offer much inducement either. In the Prussian period, Fraktur became a popular art form. Fine motifs, some of them depicting religious themes, were applied to furniture, bookplates, arithmetic exercise books, Christmas and New Year greeting cards and puzzle labyrinths. This art went well beyond the mere embellishment of key letters in a written text to floral, geometric and even animal motifs, such as deer or birds of paradise.

A distinctive Vistula Delta style of Mennonite furniture evolved, including dowry chests, bench beds, settees, wardrobes and corner cupboards. Such furniture pieces had special significance because they were normally part of the dowry when newlyweds established a new home.

Family heirlooms carried to Ukraine and subsequently to North America bear this distinct style, but after 1850, for reasons not known, the quality of Fraktur work declined. Only a few original examples can be found among Manitoba Mennonites. For the most part, however, the fine craftsmanship seen in Mennonite furniture and domestic architecture in Prussia was carried over to Ukraine and then to Canada. Early Manitoba homes were rich examples of this plain, yet tasteful functional art. There were also nice examples of carved wooden spoons, butter moulds, churns, bowls, hand mangles, carpentry tools and farm objects. Attempts have recently been made to revive this tradition by producing hobby crafts and tourists' arts, some of which are decorated with handpainted motifs. Many seniors try their hand at this after retirement.

Some ceiling frescoes of biblical scenes have been found in churches in Ukraine, but generally Mennonite churches have been kept devoid of art works. Lithographs of biblical paintings and other inspirational works were relatively common in early Canadian farm homes, sometimes as calendar art. Modestly decorative biblical inscriptions could also be found in both homes and churches.

During the last two or three decades, Mennonite fine art has evolved impressively. Artists like Wanda Koop and Aganetha Dyck have won national and international recognition. Established galleries and museums often feature these artists, as do certain Mennonite organizations. Yet some Mennonite artists do not feel accepted by their community in this role. They argue that the original injunction against art was specific to ostentatious display and should not apply to present-day art. Others ask why "a group that espouses values of community and social justice finds it difficult, if not impossible to embrace its artists." This question was put forward in the catalogue prepared for an art exhibit shown at the time of the 1990 Mennonite World Congress in Winnipeg. The curator, Priscilla Reimer, argued that Mennonite artists feel like "the insider as outsider" when they are doing their work. The irony of this is expressed by Susan Shantz, who says, "Mennonitism gave me a prototype for being 'a people apart' and the artist is often that person apart in our society."

Such arguments and sentiments have been part of the dialectic of Anabaptism since its beginning—a dialectic of conflict between individual and community values and between conservatism and innovation. At different times this cultural dynamic can be both repressive and invigorating to individuals within the community. This dynamic tension stimulates a vibrancy and commitment that has helped to perpetuate Mennonite culture and keep it vital.

ACKNOWLEDGEMENT: This paper was written while the author was Curator of Multicultural Studies at the Manitoba Museum of Man and Nature, Winnipeg.

BIBLIOGRAPHY

Abrahams, Ethel E. *Fraktur malen und Schönschreiben: The Fraktur Art and Penmanship of the Dutch German Mennonites While in Europe.* Newton, Kansas: Mennonite Press, 1980.

Bird, Michael, and Terry Kobayashi. *A Splendid Harvest: German Folk and Decorative Arts in Canada.* Toronto: Van Nostrand Reinhold, 1981.

Bodnar, John. *The Transplanted: A History of Immigrants in Urban America.* Bloomington: Indiana University Press, 1985.

Brednich, Rolf Wilhelm. *Mennonite Folklife and Folklore: A Preliminary Report. Canadian Centre for Culture Studies.* Ottawa: National Museums of Canada, 1977.

Driedger, Leo. "The Anabaptist Identification Ladder." *Mennonite Quarterly Review* 51, 4 (1977): 278–91.

———. *Mennonite Identity in Conflict.* Queenston, Ontario: Edwin Mellen Press, 1988.

———. *Mennonites in Winnipeg.* Hillsboro, Kansas: Kindred Press, 1989.

Driedger, Leo, and Leland Harder. *Anabaptist Mennonite Identities in Ferment.* Occasional Papers No. 14. Elkart, Indiana: Institute of Mennonite Studies, 1990.

Epp, Frank H. *Mennonites in Canada, 1786-1920: The History of a Separate People.* Toronto: Macmillan, 1974.

Epp, George K., and Heinrich Wiebe. *Unter dem Nordlicht: Anthology of German Mennonite Writing in Canada.* Winnipeg: Mennonite German Society of Canada, 1977.

Francis, E.K. *In Search of Utopia.* Altona, Manitoba: D.W. Friesen and Sons, 1955.

———. *Interethnic Relations: An Essay in Sociological Theory.* New York: Elsevier, 1976.

Friesen, John. *Mennonites in Russia.* Winnipeg: CMBC Publications, 1989.

Friesen, Peter M. *The Mennonite Brotherhood in Russia, 1789–1910.* Fresno, California: Board of Christian Literature, General Conference of Mennonite Brethren Churches, 1980.

Gingerich, Melvin. *Mennonite Attire through Four Centuries.* Breinegsville, Pennsylvania: Pennsylvania German Society, 1970.

Hansen, Marcus Lee, and John Bartlet Brebner. *The Mingling of the Canadian and American Peoples.* New Haven: Yale University Press, 1940.

International Songbook. Mennonite World Congress, Tenth Assembly, Lombard, Illinois, 1978.

Janzen, Reinhild K., and John M. Janzen. *Mennonite Furniture: A Migrant Tradition.* Intercourse, Pennyslvania: Good Books, 1991.

Kauffman, J. Howard, and Leo Driedger. *The Mennonite Mosaic: Identity and Modernization.* Waterloo: Herald Press, 1991.

Klassen, Doreen H. *Singing Mennonite: Low German Songs among the Mennonites.* Winnipeg: University of Manitoba Press, 1989.

Klippenstein, Lawrence, and Julius G. Toews. *Mennonite Memories: Settling Western Canada.* Winnipeg: Centennial Publications, 1977.

Loewen, Royden. "Ethnic Farmers and the 'Outside' World: Mennonites in Manitoba and Nebraska, 1874–1900." *Journal of the Canadian Historical Association* 1 (1990): 195–213.

———. "New Themes In An Old Story: Transplanted Mennonites as Group Settlers in North America, 1874–1879." *Journal of American Ethnic History* 2, 2: 3-26.

Loewen, Harry, ed. *Why I Am a Mennonite: Essays on Mennonite Identity.* Kitchener: Herald Press, 1988.

"New Mennonite Writing." *Prairie Fire* 2, 2 (Special Issue, 1990).

Redekop, John H. *A People Apart.* Winnipeg: Kindred Press, 1987.

Reimer, Alf. *"The Double Face of Mennonite Culture."* Mennonite Mirror, November 1975, 15.

Reimer, Priscilla. *Mennonite Artist: Insider as Outsider.* Winnipeg: Main/Access Gallery, 1990.

Silver, A.J. "French Canada and the Prairie Frontier." *Canadian Historical Review* 50, 1 (1969): 11–36.

Smith, C. Henry. *Smith's Story of the Mennonites.* Newton, Kansas: Faith and Life Press, 1981.

Voth, Norma Jost. *Mennonite Foods and Folkways.* 2 vols. Intercourse, Pennsylvania: Good Books, 1990–91.

Warkentin, Abe. *Strangers and Pilgrims.* Steinbach, Manitoba: Die Mennonitische Post/Derksen Printers, 1987.

MOTIF AND MESSAGE IN GERMAN-CANADIAN FOLK ART

HELGA BENNDORF TAYLOR

The decorative motifs that have been painted, carved or embroidered on cherished possessions by German-speaking immigrants and their descendants in Canada show a visible continuity with the motifs of the Old World. Even the most cursory comparison of German-Canadian folk art with the folk art of Germany, Austria and Switzerland reveals similarities in the formal attributes of most types of motif. These likenesses are evident in geometric or abstract designs as well as in representations of recognizable life forms—the phytomorphic, zoomorphic and anthropomorphic motifs that depict plants, animals and humans.

The motifs common to German folk art, whether in the Old World or the New, fulfil the same functions as artistic expression the world over. At the most general level, these include both the aesthetic function of making something more attractive and the communicative function of conveying a message. Thus, the man or woman who applies traditional motifs to everyday objects is no different from any other visual artist, of whom it has been said, "At times it is the symbolic meaning which dominates his art, at times the esthetic, but most often it is a fusion of the two."

The search for motifs that may convey specific messages is fraught with difficulties. While it is relatively easy to study the formal attributes of folk-art motifs, nonvisual aspects such as meaning can pose major challenges. This is particularly so for motifs that have been passed down for countless generations, like most of those characteristic of German-Canadian folk art. Since meaning changes over time, there is no way to know whether meanings provided by contemporary informants are the same as those of the folk artist who painted or embroidered a design one or two centuries ago. Traditional meanings, those intended by artists who are anonymous or long dead, are the most difficult to fathom.

In the absence of informant testimony, explanations of what folk art motifs meant to former generations usually rely on less direct methods of investigation. It is well to bear this in mind and to regard such explanations as suggestions or hypotheses rather than as proven facts. In seeking possible meanings for German-Canadian motifs, one source of information is the literature on Germanic folklore in Europe. It seems reasonable to assume that the German-speaking immigrants who brought their motifs to Canada would not have immediately forgotten any associated ideas and beliefs. Another source of possible meaning is the literature on the symbolism of the parent culture and its intellectual predecessors. This is particularly useful when the accepted meaning of a symbol is consistent with the context in which that symbol is used as a motif in folk art.

A good example of a motif that illustrates the latter is the ubiquitous heart, one of the most commonly used motifs of German folk artists in North America. The heart is often found in contexts that are consistent with its place as a symbol of love in European folklore. The love expressed by the heart may be romantic, declaring the sentiment of the maker or donor toward the recipient of the decorated object. This is suggested, for example, when the heart symbol is carved on a spoon intended not for eating but as a gift from a suitor to his beloved. In the same vein, hearts were sometimes embroidered on handkerchiefs that were presented by women to men. The heart could also express the love for close family members at any stage of life. The feeling of parents toward infants is demonstrated by the frequent use of the heart on cradles, as well as on birth and baptismal records and certificates. At the other end of the life cycle, the heart could express a longing for deceased family members, as suggested by its common appearance on gravemarkers in the cemeteries of German settlements in Canada.

Another motif that may have often been used to convey a symbolic message was the bird. Although some of the birds used in folk art represent existing species, such as the dove, others appear to be drawn from the imagination of the artist. A good example of the latter is the *Distelfink*, prevalent on German folk art in North America even though that European bird does not exist in the New World. The North American version of the *Distelfink* appears to be a creative invention of folk artists, based to some extent on the appearance of the goldfinch. As in mythology, birds have been used to symbolize many things in folk art, and it is difficult to know which meanings, if any, were intended for particular motifs. Context can sometimes be suggestive: for example, birds are often pictured on the bowls used in Austria to bring soup to women who have just given birth. This may be related to Indo-Germanic mythology in which birds are the bearers of life-giving drinks and to the frequent use of the bird in German fairy tales as a symbol of long and healthy life. The latter association, in particular, would be consistent with the proliferation of birds on birth and baptismal certificates prepared by German Fraktur artists in early Ontario.

Often, the message conveyed by a particular motif is intended to reinforce group values. It is not surprising that many of the motifs used by German immigrants to Canada, large numbers of whom arrived in search of religious freedom, illustrate Christian teachings. One of the most obvious references to biblical lore is the Adam-and-Eve motif, which reminds the viewer of the creation story, ever-present temptation and the consequences of sin. Adam and Eve are frequently depicted standing on either side of a tree that has a snake twining around its trunk. This particular configuration shows the tree of knowledge and not the more familiar tree of life, and the winding serpent symbolizes the devil. Not all references to biblical themes or Christian teachings are as explicitly representational as Adam and Eve or the serpent. For example, it has been suggested that folk artists in Germany have used the three-tipped tulip as a variation of the Holy Lily to symbolize the Trinity.

Another motif with presumably religious overtones is the familiar tree of life. Often this motif takes the shape of branches or stems of flowers in a vase. Tree-of-life motifs are well known in the Austrian, German and Swiss Alps, northern Germany and German settlements in North America. They are embroidered on show towels and samplers and painted or carved on chests and wardrobes. The tree has been described as a symbol of inexhaustible life and, therefore, immortality. Also, reaching from deep in the earth into heaven, the tree of life links the different worlds of heaven and earth. Through its association with Paradise, it sometimes signifies regeneration and a return to the primordial state of perfection.

In some cases, the message of the motif may be directed at nonhuman agents. Folklorists have identified several motifs in German folk art that have been used as protection against misfortune, presumably by communicating their symbolic message to the evil spirits that plague mankind. A good example is the rooster, whose distinctive behaviour has made him the symbol of various qualities. Among these are vigilance, as exhibited by his loud calls at dawn. As a motif on weather vanes, the rooster appears to watch for evil in all directions. When this notion is combined with the aggression so characteristic of roosters, it is not surprising to find that the rooster has emerged in Christian teaching as a symbol of victory over evil. In Austria, the rooster on church towers and weather vanes was thought to ward off evil as well as to protect the surrounding settlement from lightning and bad storms.

A protective function has also been suggested for some of the many stars that are common in German and German-Canadian folk art. The five-pointed star, known as *Drudenfuß* in Austria and Germany, was often carved into the ridge purlins of houses and barns because of its power to ward off evil. The six-pointed star has been accorded the power to curb rebellious spirits and ward off danger. One form of six-pointed star is composed of two equilateral triangles, while another, the compass star, is made up of circle segments drawn with a compass.

A specialized application of the star motif in North America was a symbol painted on barns by German-speaking settlers in Pennsylvania and popularly known as a hex sign. The hex sign displayed remarkable variation in form and colour, but typically comprised a circle that had different stars or other motifs within its circumference. Though there has been considerable debate over the significance of the hex sign, there is testimonial evidence that it once functioned to protect the barn from lightning and to keep the animals from being bewitched, or *ferhexed*. Although German-Canadians did not decorate their barns with hex signs, similar designs have been used on many smaller objects. These include sailcloth mats from Lunenburg County, Nova Scotia, which were placed in front of sailors' bunks aboard ships.

Folk-art motifs also commemorate or celebrate major stages in the life cycle. For example, in the Austrian Alps, the rose, either portrayed in a naturalistic way or as a rosette, was a common motif on wedding furniture, including dowry chests. The flowers may have represented the bride herself, deriving symbolic meaning from the association of roses with the Virgin Mary in the fine arts and music of the Baroque period and earlier. Another motif that was sometimes painted on wedding furniture in the Austrian Alps was a young couple. This has been described as a symbol of the rebirth of Adam and Eve, just married and starting a new family in their own Paradise, namely their farmstead.

In seeking to understand the messages conveyed by folk-art motifs, it is important to remember that symbolic content, like any other aspect of culture, can and does change over time. Change can be sudden and dramatic, as perhaps best exemplified by the now infamous swastika. The word *swastika* is derived from the Sanskrit *svasti*, meaning well-being. From ancient times this motif conveyed a message of friendliness. As long as it remained a symbol of goodwill, German folk artists in both Europe and Canada used the swastika and its variant, the swirling swastika with curvilinear arms, to decorate embroidery, furniture and small containers. After the swastika was appropriated by the Nazi party in the early twentieth century, it immediately became an international symbol of racial intolerance.

The message conveyed by most motifs does not change as rapidly as this. Nevertheless, many of the meanings that were appropriate in the peasant societies of former times are no longer valid in the modern world. Although contemporary folk artists may value the old motifs more for their decorative value than for their traditional meaning, the communicative function of traditional motifs has not completely lost out to their aesthetic function. Even the German-Canadians who claim to use the old motifs "just for nice" are still conveying a message to the viewer: By continuing to use the same motifs as their forebears, they are communicating a pride in their ethnic heritage for all to see.

BIBLIOGRAPHY

Arthur, Eric, and Dudley Witney. *The Barn*. Toronto: M.F. Feheley Arts Co. Ltd., 1972.

Cirlot, J.E. *A Dictionary of Symbols*. New York: Philosophical Library Inc., 1962.

Cooper, J.C. *An Illustrated Encyclopedia of Traditional Symbols*. New York: Thames and Hudson Inc., 1990.

Gephart, Kay. *Painting Hex Signs "Chust For Nice."* Annandale, Virginia: Charles Baptie Studios, 1973.

Jobes, Gertrude. *Dictionary of Mythology, Folklore and Symbols*. 3 vols. New York: The Scarecrow Press Inc., 1962.

Kaufmann, Paul. *Brauchtum in Österreich*. Vienna and Hamburg: Paul Zsolny Verlag, 1982.

Knobler, Nathan. *The Visual Dialogue: An Introduction to the Appreciation of Art*. New York: Holt, Rinehart and Winston, 1966.

Mahr, August C. "Origin and Significance of Pennsylvania Dutch Barn Symbols." In *The Study of Folklore*. Ed. Alan Dundes. Englewood Cliffs: Prentice Hall, Inc., 1965.

Reaman, G. Elmore. "Folklore, Folk Art and Characteristic Foods of the Province of Ontario." *German-Canadian Yearbook*. Toronto: Historical Society of Mecklenburg Upper Canada Inc., 1973.

Schmidt, Leopold. *Volkskunst in Österreich*. Vienna: Forum Verlag, 1966.

Zwittnig, Katharina. *Das Tier im Volksglauben und Brauch: Die Vögel. Volkskunst Heute*, Jg.7, Heft 3. Vienna: Heimatwerk in Österreich, 1988.

From the Collections

NOTE: "CCFCS" refers to the Canadian Centre for Folk Culture Studies, a research division of the Canadian Museum of Civilization, and "HIS" refers to the Museum's History Division. The sizes for all pieces are given from the largest to the smallest dimension for two reasons: First, the measurements are different enough that it is clear which dimensions are larger. Second, some pieces could be viewed from a choice of angles, making "length" or "width" descriptions arbitrary.

Chests

Chests used for storage and safekeeping are often painted with decorations, while those used for transportation are usually plain or decorated with metalwork. A girl's hope chest contained linen and bedding, which she would need for her married life. As chests could easily be outfitted with locks, they were relatively safe places to store valuables and were ideal for carrying an emigrant's belongings on the long journey to a new land.

CHEST
Pennsylvania or Ontario
1801
Wood
135.9 x 70 x 65.6 cm
CCFCS 71-177

This chest has moulding around the lid and base, and painted designs on the front. Marked "Lind 1801," it might have been used as a hope chest or blanket box.

CHEST
Michael S. Schmiedel
Berlin, Germany
1791
Oak, iron
115 x 67.5 x 67 cm
CCFCS 71-176

This chest was used by the artisan's son when he immigrated to Pennsylvania in 1859, and later to Waterloo County in 1861. The ironwork, typical of the second half of the eighteenth century, was for decoration as well as structural reinforcement.

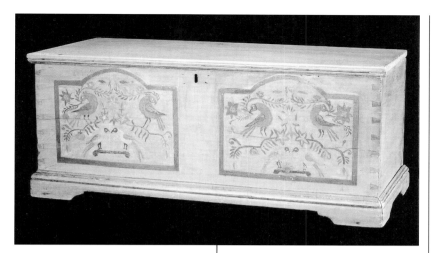

CHEST
Ontario
Wood
103 x 48 x 44.5 cm
CCFCS 79-475

This waxed, natural-wood chest has dovetail joints and a hinged lid, which is missing some of its moulding on the right side. Legs extend from the moulding on the base. The painted front panels bear the traditional German symbols of tulips and pairs of birds.

CHEST
Saskatchewan
Pre-1922
Wood, metal
92 x 51 x 48 cm
CCFCS 72-683

This trunk carried the belongings of Mennonites who migrated from Saskatchewan to Mexico in 1922–23. It was later brought back to Canada by another family. The multicoloured, traditional designs that adorn the natural wood are not the original ones, but were made at a later date in Warman, Saskatchewan. The top and front are the most highly decorated, with designs of birds and flowers. The inscription "GEMACHT IM JAHRE 1865" (made in 1865) appears on the top, and "1865" is repeated on the front. There is a scroll design around the ends of the handles.

CHEST
Nova Scotia
Eighteenth century
Pine, iron
87.5 x 38 x 32 cm
CCFCS 74-339

This small chest with dovetail joints is partitioned to divide the interior into two different-size compartments. The two medallions on the front, outlined in chip-carving, enclose portraits of women in eighteenth-century European clothing. However, their head coverings of feathers (or leaves) are suggestive of Native North Americans. An escutcheon design on the lid, also outlined in chip-carving, surrounds a vase filled with tulips. This is a variation of the tree-of-life motif, also referred to as the "flower-in-pot" motif. The simple hinges and lock are hand-forged, suggesting that the chest may have been made at an earlier date than the painted decoration. Chests like this were used to store valuables, important papers and sometimes the family Bible.

Wardrobes & Cupboards

A *Kleiderschrank* is a type of wardrobe which originated in seventeenth-century Germany. It was brought from the Palatinate (southwest Germany) to Pennsylvania, and from there to Ontario. Despite its size, it could be transported easily because it was constructed in separate sections and could be quickly disassembled. These wardrobes, usually with two long doors, often included shelves, one or two drawers and fitted pegs on which to hang clothes.

WARDROBE
John P. Klemp
Hanover, Ontario
ca. 1885
Cherry, maple, walnut
229 x 175.5 x 52.6 cm

HIS 978.17.1

This large *Kleiderschrank* with two drawers is elaborately inlaid with maple and walnut in the Continental German tradition. The cabinetmaker to whom this is attributed, John P. Klemp, was a German Canadian.

CORNER CUPBOARD
Hepburn, Saskatchewan
ca. 1910
Wood, brass
153.8 x 85 x 49 cm
CCFCS 71-237

Small corner cupboards were typical Mennonite furnishings in western Canada. This model is stained and varnished, rather than painted, and has a three-sided front with a gracefully curved pediment.

CORNER CUPBOARD
Kitchener, Ontario
Late nineteenth century
Wood, metal, porcelain
115 x 68 x 40 cm
CCFCS 77-679

The hinged door of this Mennonite cupboard has a floral cutout print glued to its centre, and the peaked pediment (gable) is decorated with a star. Two of the three drawers have porcelain knobs. The short feet are turned. This cupboard was handed down in a family by the name of Friesen.

CORNER CUPBOARD
Saskatchewan
Nineteenth century
Wood, metal, porcelain
91.5 x 62 x 40 cm
CCFCS 77-441

This stained and varnished Mennonite cupboard has a beautiful inlaid frieze with the inscription "A M." On the side are more inlays, both floral (the "flower-in-pot" motif, a widely known decorative design in the German-Canadian community) and geometric. The side columns are three-quarter turned. The two drawers have porcelain knobs.

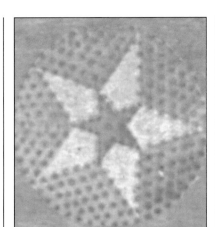

PIE SAFE
Ontario
Nineteenth century
Wood, tin, brass
172.8 x 103 x 43 cm

CCFCS 74-210

Although rare today, pie safes were once common among Ontarians of Germanic origin (via Pennsylvania). The perforated tin panels recessed into the doors allowed air to circulate around the freshly baked goods while keeping out pests. Blue, yellow, green and brown were used to paint the stars, diamonds, circles and flowers on the upper and lower doors. The knobs are brass.

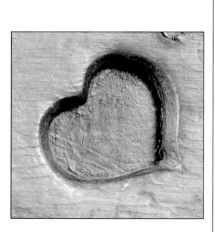

DISH DRESSER
August Boehme
Palmer Rapids, Ontario
Nineteenth century
Wood
188.2 x 107 x 55 cm

CCFCS 81-421

This dish dresser is made in the German vernacular tradition. The elegantly curved pediment and sides of the top section contrast with the simply carved rosettes and cutout hearts of the bottom. The dresser is attributed to August Boehme (see biographical sketch).

Tables & Seating

TABLE
Waterloo County, Ontario
ca. 1850
Pine
150 x 97 x 75 cm
CCFCS 85-1981

This peg-top table, in a typical early Pennsylvania-German style, is attributed to Abraham Latschaw (1799–1870), a Mennonite cabinet-maker from Berks County, Pennsylvania, who moved to Mannheim, Waterloo County, in 1822 (see biographical sketch). The original ochre colour has been preserved. The table is accompanied by a matching bench, also in the CMC collection; matching sets rarely survive together for more than a few generations.

DESK
Hastings, Ontario
ca. 1870
Wood, metal, leather
165.6 x 128.5 x 96 cm
CCFCS 75-1159

This stationmaster's desk has a label on the back which reads "Canadian Express Co." On the side is the saying "Go to the ant thou sluggard" (Proverbs 6:6), telling the reader to look to the ant as an example of diligence. The desk top has a leather insert, and the sides and doors are decorated with German folk-art motifs (vases, tulips, hearts) in green, yellow, blue, black and red.

DRY SINK
Ontario
Nineteenth century
Wood, metal, glass
119 x 78.5 x 45.5 cm

CCFCS 78-271

Dry sinks are often found in areas of Ontario settled by people of German descent. This Mennonite model has a built-in basin, a small drawer and two hinged doors. It is made of pine, walnut and mahogany, and the front panels are richly decorated with birds and flowers. The glass pull knobs fit badly and are clearly not the originals. This dry sink is from the estate of Mrs. E. Clemmer of Hanover, Western Ontario.

SETTLE
Germanicus (Renfrew), Ontario
Late nineteenth century
Wood
82 x 64 x 57 cm

CCFCS 75-1361

The settle, a seat intended for two or more people, originated in the late Middle Ages (Europe, 1100–1500). In North America, cabinetmakers often enclosed the legs and hinged the seat to create storage space. The bench shown here came from Robert Raglan's farm which has been in the family for three generations. The shaping of the back and arms, as well as the compass stars carved into the backrest, are typically German.

MILKING STOOL
John Waldner
Hutterville Colony, Alberta
Twentieth century
Wood
36.5 x 31 x 24.5 cm

CCFCS 71-193

This octagonal milking stool was
made by John Waldner, the Hutterville
Colony carpenter. A handle was
added for easy lifting.

CHAIR
August Boehme
Palmer Rapids, Ontario
Nineteenth century
Wood
82 x 50 x 38 cm

CCFCS 82-154

A chair with a heart cut out of the
backrest for easy lifting is a form
widespread in Germany and
Austria. This side chair, which was
originally green, is dowel-joined
and has round, splayed legs.
Family tradition attributes the chair
to August Boehme, who emigrated
from Brandenburg to the Ottawa
Valley in 1865 (see biographical
sketch).

Mats & Rugs

Painting sailcloth mats was a nineteenth-century East Coast folk-art tradition. Sailors placed these mats in front of their bunk or hammock aboard ship. Mats with fringes were probably used as wall decorations. Decorated sailcloth mats are still found in homes in Lunenburg County.

MAT
Lunenburg County, Nova Scotia
ca. 1900
Canvas, oil paint
104 x 56 cm

CCFCS 81-315

The handshake motif, common on Maritime sailcloth mats, represented the spiritual connection between the sailor and his loved ones left behind on shore.

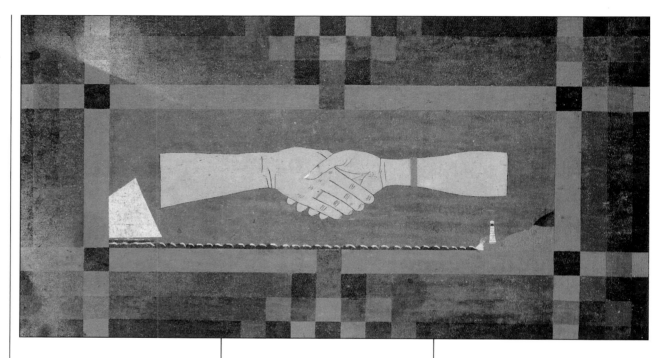

MAT
Lunenburg, Nova Scotia
1890–1910
Sailcloth, oil paint
126 x 56 cm

CCFCS 82-18

The tree-of-life motif, common to the traditional art of many cultures, was often changed in German folk art to flowers in a pot.

RUG
H. Fry
Mount Forest, Ontario
1960–1975
Burlap, felt
187 x 65 cm

CCFCS 78-272

This Mennonite hooked rug of multi-coloured felt strips shows an outdoor scene: a house surrounded by trees; a path leading from the house to a bridge crossing the stream; a deer jumping over a fence; grey mountains; and a setting sun. Backed by burlap, this rug has never been used.

RUG
Mrs. Niessen
Warman, Saskatchewan
1970
Cotton, wool, burlap
180 x 89 cm

CCFCS 74-317

Working from time to time throughout one full winter, Mrs. Niessen, a Mennonite, turned old rags into this beautiful hooked rug with a colourful floral motif. She dyed all the materials herself (except for some of the greys).

Beds & Bedding

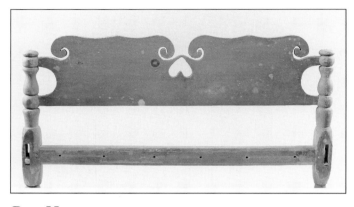

BED HEADBOARD
New Germany, Nova Scotia
Early nineteenth century
Wood
120.5 x 75.6 cm
CCFCS 74-407

This green headboard features turned posts and is carved with a cutout heart and curve designs. Its short legs allow it to fit under sloping ceilings.

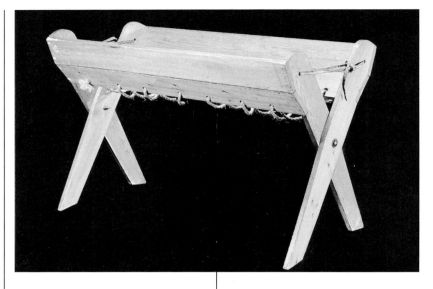

FOLDING CRADLE
Wood, rope
106.7 x 63.5 cm
CCFCS 71-185

The legs of this Russian-made Hutterite cradle are attached scissor-fashion to the side boards for easy folding. The bottom is made of rope lacings. It came from Russia to Saskatoon via a Hutterite colony in North Dakota.

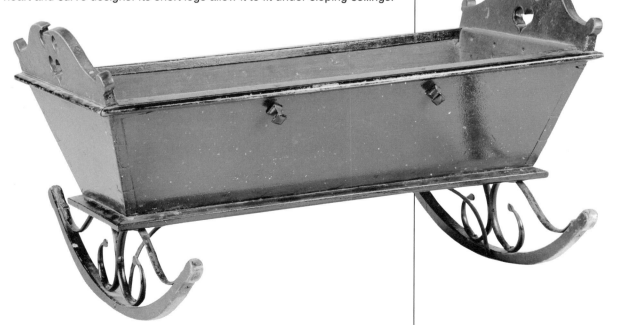

CRADLE
ca. 1900
Wood, metal
92 x 77.5 x 51 cm
CCFCS 78-416

This open cradle has dovetail joints, curved end boards and wrought-iron rockers. The decorative heart-shaped cutouts also serve as handholds, and are perhaps a sign of affection. Of Russian Mennonite origin, this cradle is typical of those found in Mennonite settlements in Manitoba and Saskatchewan.

QUILT
Ontario
1935–1945
Cotton
204 x 176 cm

CCFCS 84-11

A typical quilt consists of three layers stitched together: the decorated upper side, the warm filling, and the backing. Quilting spread west from China to Europe via the Middle East. The Pilgrims brought quilts to the New World in 1620. To protect its monopoly on the textile market, England forbade American colonists to produce their own woven cloth (and even refused weavers permission to emigrate). This situation created a need which was admirably filled by the quilt. Only imagination and some scraps of recycled cloth were needed to make an artistic and functionally superior substitute for woven bed-covers. Quilting thus came into its own in America. As other, non-English, immigrants arrived, they adopted the technique but used the decorative motifs of their own homelands. Pennsylvania-German quilts are known for their brilliant colours and detailed patterns—often of tulips and other flowers.

This Mennonite quilt in black, brown and beige has a centre formed of small and large diamonds. The back is lined with blue cotton, and there is very little batting. The quilt was made in the Shetler family.

BEDSPREAD
J. Witmer
Lancaster County, Pennsylvania
1838
Linen, wool
228.6 x 167.7 cm

CCFCS 71-477

The name, place and date are woven into this spread. The lengthwise yarns (warp) are linen, and the widthwise yarns (weft, or woof) are wool. The design of birds and flowers is typically German.

Wall Pieces

MIRROR
Lunenburg, Nova Scotia
Early twentieth century
Wood, glass
32.5 x 32 x 2 cm
CCFCS 77-166

The maker of this colourful wooden plaque declared his Christian values with the traditional symbols for faith (the cross), hope (the anchor) and charity (the heart).

SPICE CABINET
Saskatchewan
Wood, brass
41 x 23 x 10.5 cm
CCFCS 74-304

This eight-drawer cabinet with brass pulls and gracefully curved pediment was made in or near the Old Colony Mennonite village of Blumenthal.

SPOON BOARD
Southern Ontario
Wood
38.4 x 17 x 3.8 cm
CCFCS 73-616

In Germany, it used to be said of a poor home, "There isn't a spoon on the wall there." However, an elaborate display of spoons in a decorated holder indicated that nobody in that household was in want of anything. This spoon board, similar to the type from Lower Saxony, has two narrow shelves with holes for three spoons each, a pointed top, a scalloped bottom and multicoloured floral designs.

WASHBASIN HOLDER
Manitoba(?)
Wood, metal
102.9 x 47.9 x 41.2 cm
CCFCS 77-269.1-2

This wall-mounted Hutterite washbasin holder was collected at Headingley, Manitoba. The top shelf is held to the varnished wooden backboard with curved brackets. The two recessed panels have bevelled edges. The basin holder is attached to the wooden frame with a metal latch and sliding hinge.

Show Towels

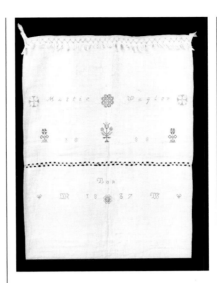

E mbroidered by young women before their marriage, often in their early teens, show towels were hung in front of the everyday towel to hide it. For centuries, the motifs of flowers, hearts, vases and birds, usually done in cross-stitch, remained the same. In the eighteenth century, the alphabet, numbers, trees, plants and animals became predominant, together with symbols of marriage: Adam and Eve, and couples holding hands. Often, the artist added her name and the date. This tradition was continued in the New World.

SHOW TOWEL
Waterloo, Ontario
1825
Linen, cotton
135 x 43 cm

CCFCS 83-958

This white linen towel with a knotted fringe is embroidered with flowers in red cotton cross-stitch. Other motifs—geometric shapes, flowers, birds and hearts—are executed in a technique known as drawn work: some of the threads of warp and woof are removed, or drawn out, to form patterns. "F.B.A.L. 1825" are perhaps the artist's initials and date of completion.

SHOW TOWEL
Mattie Wagler
Ontario
1888
Linen, cotton
116 x 42 cm

CCFCS 83-959

"Mattie Wagler 1888 from M.1837" is cross-stitched in cotton on this linen towel.

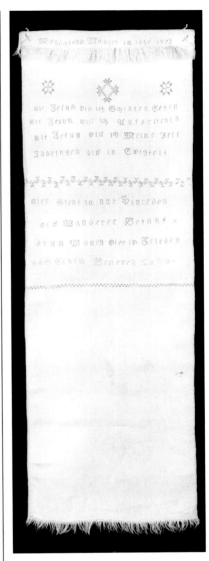

SHOW TOWEL
Magdalena Wagner
Waterloo, Ontario
1872
Linen
132.1 x 43.2 cm

CCFCS 74-200

A Mennonite girl embroidered the religious text, diamond and star into this white linen towel in red and green threads, and dated her work "1872."

Boxes & Baskets

SMALL CHEST
Saskatchewan
First half, twentieth century
Wood, brass
62 x 38.5 x 31 cm
CCFCS 72-684

This small varnished chest with dovetailed corners was made by a Mennonite. Two of the four legs are turned on a lathe. It has a hinged lid and a keyhole with fancy brass trim.

SMALL CHEST
Peter Hofer
Beiseker, Alberta
ca. 1955
Wood
48.3 x 28 x 21.6 cm
CCFCS 71-232

Peter Hofer was the carpenter of the Hutterite Rosebud Colony near Beiseker, Alberta. He made this small chest for Annie Tschetter, who used it as a sewing chest at the Riverview Colony in Saskatchewan. Constructed with nails, the chest has a hinged lid and decorative woodwork covering the corners. The whole chest is highly varnished, with the moulding framing the lid and base. The initials "A.T." on the front are surrounded by flowers and foliage in green and red. Inside, the chest is painted yellow. On the left is a small compartment with lid.

SMALL CHEST
Peter Hofer
Beiseker, Alberta
ca. 1950
Wood
43.2 x 24.2 x 26.7 cm
CCFCS 71-233

Peter Hofer made this sewing chest for Rosie Tschetter. It has four feet, rounded corners and a hinged lid. The initials "R.T." on the front are surrounded by floral designs in yellow, red and green. All nails are carefully covered, and the chest is varnished inside and out.

BENTWOOD BOX
1820–1840
Wood
46.8 x 28.5 cm
CCFCS 74-272

Found near Ottawa, this German box is signed with the initials "C K"

inside a heart. On the sides are multicoloured floral motifs; the lid shows a monk sitting between two trees. The rhymed inscription in German translates as: "Here in this solitude, I live in contentment."

FOOT WARMER
Southern Ontario or Pennsylvania
Early nineteenth century
Wood, brass
23 x 19 x 18 cm
CCFCS 77-153

In Germany, women took foot warmers to church to keep their feet cosy during long services. The warmers were often produced by artisans rather than carpenters. This box-shaped model is richly painted with multicoloured floral, human and animal motifs. The perforations on the sides and top, in a gothic rosette pattern, permit the warmth to reach the user's feet. The panel at the front slides to allow heating materials to be put inside. This foot warmer came from the Stortenbecher family, who moved from Pennsylvania to settle in Thornhill, Ontario. It is not known whether they brought the warmer with them or had it made in Ontario.

BENTWOOD BOX
Mid-nineteenth century
Spruce
46.3 x 29.8 x 17.8 cm
CCFCS 73-648

This hand-painted German box was brought to Pennsylvania around 1860. The multicoloured design includes a family scene on the lid, with the inscription, "Der Klapperstorch hat vergangne Nacht einen kleinen Bruder Euch gebracht." (The stork brought you a little brother last night.)

STORAGE BOX
Owen Sound, Ontario
Nineteenth century
Wood
51 x 42 x 35.5 cm
CCFCS 74-284

This Mennonite box with its hinged, sloping lid was probably used to store the family Bible. The back, extending beyond the sides, is decorated with double curves and scrolls. Carved on the front are traditional designs: birds, whirling sun, fish and hearts.

CUTLERY BOX
St. Jacobs, Ontario
Wood
31.5 x 24.3 x 17.9 cm
CCFCS 81-327

This Mennonite cutlery box has hinged lids and a handle on top. The outside is painted brown and green in floral motifs; the inside is unpainted.

DOCUMENT BOX
Cambridge, Ontario
Nineteenth century
Tin
24 x 20 x 15.5 cm
CCFCS 71-179

Document boxes were used in many countries, but the shape and decoration of this one are typical of Pennsylvania Germans, who brought their traditions to southern Ontario. This type of toleware box was made by a tinsmith, sometimes known as a "whitesmith." The box shown here has a rounded lid and small wire handle, and is decorated with multicoloured floral designs.

SEWING BOX
Saskatchewan
Early twentieth century
Wood, lacquer
18.5 x 14 x 13.5 cm

CCFCS 77-129

Painted black with coloured floral designs, this Mennonite sewing box also features much decorative carving. It has an upper compartment with a lid, a small drawer in the centre and four delicately carved feet.

BASKET
Jacob Wipf
Magrath, Alberta
ca. 1962
Willow
55.9 x 38.2 cm

CCFCS 71-194

This oval basket was used to carry laundry. The horizontal stripes and some vertical staves are painted.

BASKET
David Waldner
Magrath, Alberta
ca. 1945
Willow
55 cm (diam.) x 33 cm

CCFCS 71-195

Dark and light willows are woven in horizontal stripes around thirty-two vertical staves in this two-handled potato basket. The scrap willows used for the stand can be replaced separately.

Kerchiefs

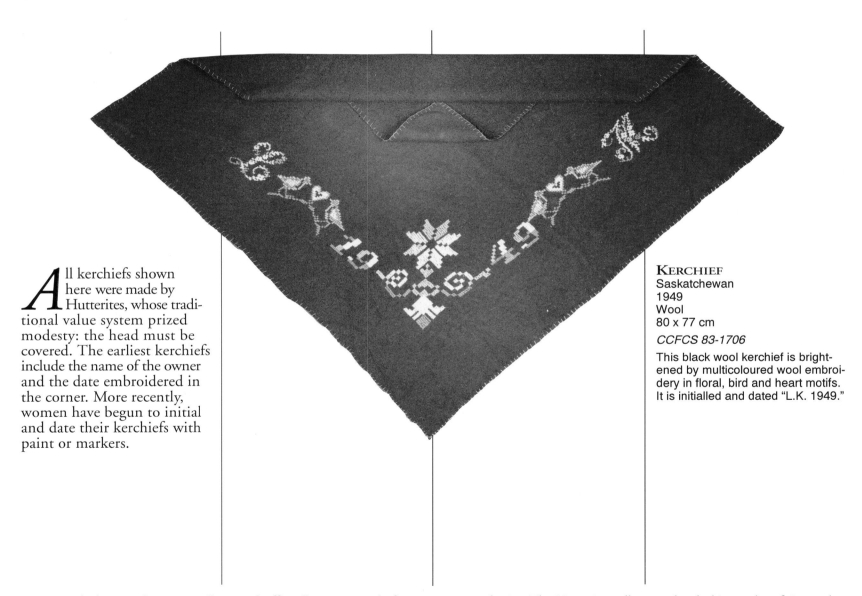

KERCHIEF
Saskatchewan
1949
Wool
80 x 77 cm
CCFCS 83-1706
This black wool kerchief is brightened by multicoloured wool embroidery in floral, bird and heart motifs. It is initialled and dated "L.K. 1949."

A ll kerchiefs shown here were made by Hutterites, whose traditional value system prized modesty: the head must be covered. The earliest kerchiefs include the name of the owner and the date embroidered in the corner. More recently, women have begun to initial and date their kerchiefs with paint or markers.

NOTE: Clothing in this section, "Personal Effects," comes mostly from Hutterite colonies. The Hutterites adhere to the clothing styles of sixteenth-century Switzerland and Tyrol. They originally avoided buttons in favour of hooks to distance themselves from the military and to emphasize their pacifist beliefs. In the European homelands, soldiers' uniforms were replete with buttons. (Moustaches, another military fashion, were likewise eschewed.)

KERCHIEF
Katie Waldner
Poplar Point, Manitoba
Pre-1977
Cotton, paint
80 x 35 cm

CCFCS 77-426

The maker of this black cotton kerchief with white dots painted her name in one corner in yellow, green and blue.

KERCHIEF
Katie Hofer
Poplar Point, Manitoba
1926
Cotton
60 x 55 cm

CCFCS 77-424

This black cotton kerchief, dotted with white, is embroidered with the owner's name and date in one corner.

KERCHIEF
Annie Waldner
Poplar Point, Manitoba
1948
Wool, cotton
93 x 93 cm

CCFCS 77-420

This black wool head scarf is fringed with wool on two sides. The floral embroidery in one corner is cross-stitched in cotton, as are the owner's name and the date: "Annie 1948 Waldner."

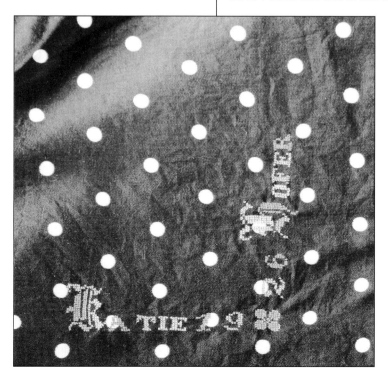

Clothing & Accessories

WOMAN'S SUN HAT
Rebecca Wipf
Magrath, Alberta
ca. 1963
Cotton, wood
45 x 30 cm
CCFCS 71-1136

Bonnets like this one of striped cotton were used by Hutterite women working in the garden. The back flap protected the neck, and the large sun visor, stiffened with wooden ribs, shielded the face.

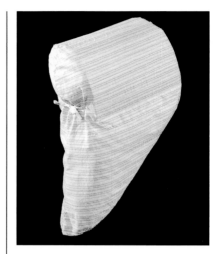

WOMAN'S SUN HAT
Rachel Wollman
Leask, Saskatchewan
ca. 1950
Cotton, wood
45 x 26 cm
CCFCS 77-813

This bonnet of brown print on white cotton was machine sewn, and stiffened with wooden ribs. Donated by the maker.

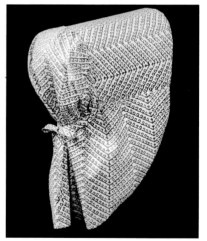

WOMAN'S ENSEMBLE
Rebecca Wipf
Magrath, Alberta
ca. 1963
Cotton
Top: 47 x 43 cm; sleeve: 46 cm
Skirt: 93 x 106 cm
CCFCS 71-1131, 71-1132

The skirt and top are both made of printed cotton.

WOMAN'S SUN HAT
Poplar Point, Manitoba
Pre-1977
Cotton, wood
45 x 29 cm
CCFCS 77-428

The traditional polka-dot pattern is brightened by a red cotton print lining. Fine wooden ribs stiffen the visor.

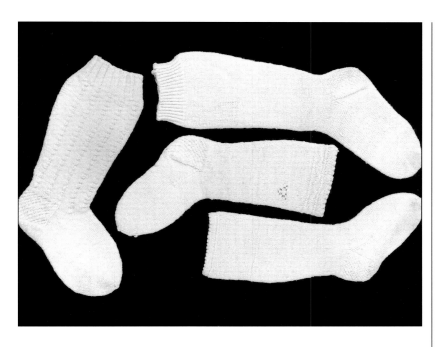

MEN'S SOCKS
Saskatchewan
Mid-twentieth century
Wool

These four pairs of socks were all made for the preacher-manager of the Riverview Colony, Mike Stahl. Because the Hutterites practise communal living, nothing is owned personally; only by initialling and dating an item could it be given as a special present. These socks are thus all suitably labelled.

45 x 25 cm

CCFCS 83-1697

Socks with a cuff-type finish, initialled "M ST 1954."

38 x 24 cm

CCFCS 83-1695

Socks with a cuff-type finish, initialled "S."

36 x 23 cm
CCFCS 83-1700

Socks with a zig-zag motif finish, initialled "F A."

36 x 21 cm

CCFCS 83-1701

Socks with a diamond motif finish, initialled "R ST."

WALKING STICK
Simon Gascho
New Hamburg, Ontario
1870–1890
Wood, brass
90 cm

CCFCS 77-159

Walking sticks are often carved with the motif of a serpent winding around the shaft, perhaps because it lends itself to the shape. The motif may also refer to the story of Adam and Eve. The top of this neatly carved stick was turned on a lathe. A brass cap protects the base.

COWBOY CHAPS
Minneapolis area, United States
ca. 1917
Sheepskin, cotton
97 x 53 cm

CCFCS 79-821

This pair of chaps was made in a Minnesota Hutterite colony early in this century and then brought to the Swift Current Colony in Saskatchewan. The cloth legs, each with five clasps, are lined with sheepskin. Held up by a leather belt and buckle the chaps are dyed black in keeping with Hutterite clothing traditions, which largely avoid colour and emphasize modesty and unworldliness.

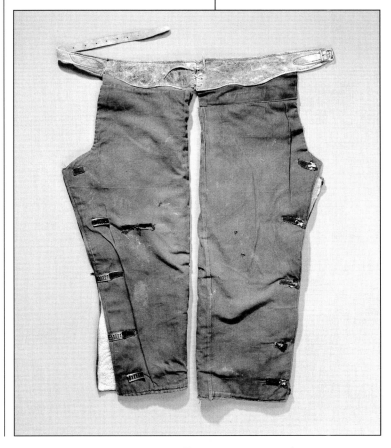

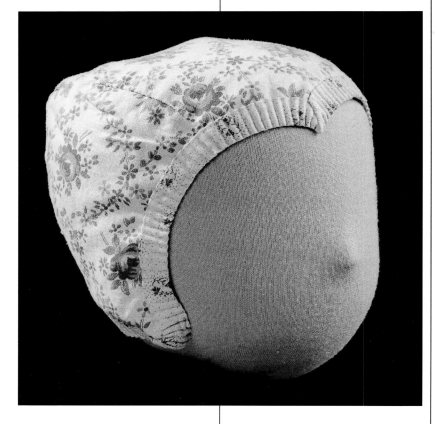

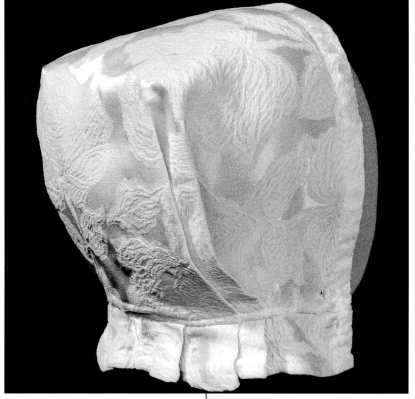

GIRL'S CAP
Rachel Wollman
Leask, Saskatchewan
ca. 1950
Cotton
14 x 11 cm

CCFCS 77-815

A floral pattern of roses, with chequered cotton lining, was chosen for this girl's cap. Donated by the maker.

BOY'S CAP
Russia
Flannel, wool
20 x 16 cm

CCFCS 77-802

This black cloth Hutterite cap is enlivened with chequered flannel lining, burgundy ribbon trim, and a red-and-blue wool tassel. Donated by Susie Stahl.

GIRL'S CAP
R. Wipf
Magrath, Alberta
ca. 1965
Cotton and silk satin
21 x 14 cm

CCFCS 71-1150

This skull cap with creases at the back was made for a little girl. The two ribbons are for tying it under the chin.

Presentation Handkerchiefs

Handkerchiefs as tokens of love and friendship have a long history in southern Germany and Austria: examples are preserved from the sixteenth century. Betrothed men and women carried specially embroidered handkerchiefs. Hutterites continued this tradition in the present century. (For more information on presentation handkerchiefs, see the article by Robert Klymasz in this volume.)

HANDKERCHIEF
Poplar Point, Manitoba
1926
Cotton
41 x 41 cm

CCFCS 77-433

This white cotton square is embroidered with red and white cherries in one corner. The embroidered script in German and English reads, "Forget me not, Joseph Waldner."

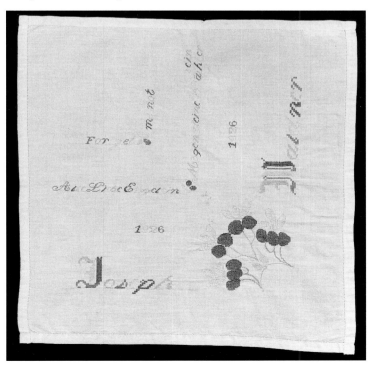

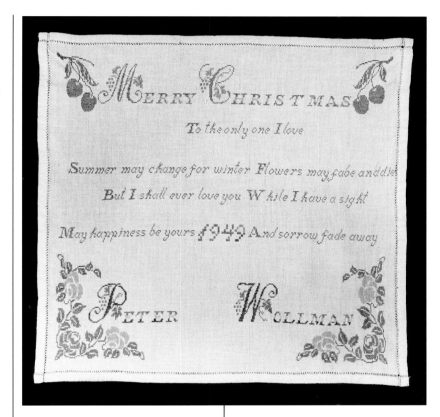

HANDKERCHIEF
Poplar Point, Manitoba
1949
Cotton
42 x 42 cm

CCFCS 77-432

This white cotton square is embroidered with cross-stitch flowers in multicoloured cotton thread. A Christmas greeting is embroidered in the centre.

HANDKERCHIEF
Victoria, Ontario
First half, twentieth century
Cotton
39 x 35 cm

CCFCS 78-87

The phrase stitched in colourful cotton
thread on a white cotton panel says,
"May you always be together. Good
luck. Joseph Waldner."

HANDKERCHIEF
Barbara Hofer
Arm River Colony, Saskatchewan
Pre-1978
Cotton
43 x 43 cm

CCFCS 78-543

The inscription embroidered on this
white cotton square says,
"Somebody Loves You. May Your
Life Be Bright. Barbara Hofer.
Joseph Wollman."

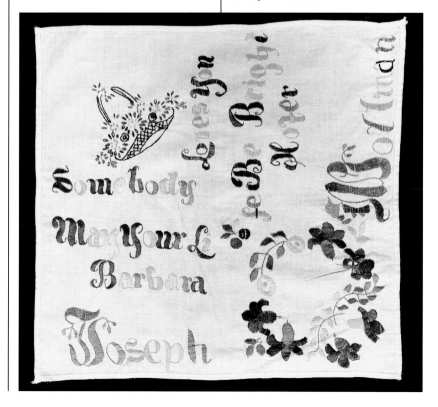

Textile Work

WOOL WINDER
Lunenburg County, Nova Scotia
Nineteenth century
Birch wood
89 x 75 x 22 cm

CCFCS 84-405

The base of this wool winder is raised
on four short legs. The vertical board
has scalloped edges, and punched
and painted decorations. The four
rotating arms hold the wool.

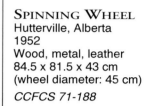

WOOL WINDER (NIDDY-NODDY)
Charles Thom,
Poltimore, Quebec
ca. 1880
Wood
57 x 33 cm

CCFCS 84-159

Winders of this type were the earliest devices developed to skein newly
spun wool. The wool was measured by twisting and turning motions, with
the operator counting the turns until the required amount was wound. This
winder was made from local wood by Charles Thom, an emigrant from
Germany. Roughly hewn T-bars are set at right angles to each other at
either end of the shaft.

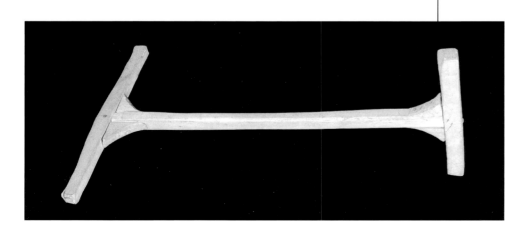

SPINNING WHEEL
Hutterville, Alberta
1952
Wood, metal, leather
84.5 x 81.5 x 43 cm
(wheel diameter: 45 cm)

CCFCS 71-188

This elaborate wheel made in the
double-drive style has lathe-turned
spokes, legs, and spindle and
wheel supports; a leather-hinged
treadle and a stationary treadle bar;
a sloped saddle; and glossy yellow
painted wood with a floral motif on
the base in yellow, red and green.
An inscription on the rear of the
saddle indicates that this was the
seventeenth model made by J.M. in
1952. A spinning wheel was often
given to a Hutterite bride by her
parent colony.

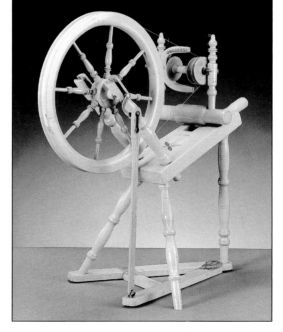

FLAX COMB
Waterloo County, Ontario
Eighteenth century
Wood, iron
63.7 x 16.3 x 13 cm

CCFCS 79-1612

This comb, used to separate and straighten flax fibres as well as remove rough particles before spinning, is typical of Ontario Germans. Its round cluster of iron spikes is mounted on a shaped board that features punched decorations.

MANGLE AND ROLLER
Alberta
1915
Wood
Mangle: 67 x 9.5 x 4 cm
Roller: 49 x 6 cm (diam.)

CCFCS 74-533(1.2)

To remove water and wrinkles from linen and other flat laundry, the fabric was wrapped around a roller and then pressed and rubbed with a smooth or corrugated mangle board. A necessity in every bride's trousseau, mangles were widely used throughout Europe. The set shown here was brought to Canada by Hutterites. Whereas the roller was turned on a lathe, the mangle was carved from one piece of wood, with a turned handle attached. The compass-drawn rosette on the mangle is a typical decoration. The initials "EKH" and the date "1915" are also incised.

FLAX COMB
Alberta
Wood, iron
97 x 40 x 3.5 cm

CCFCS 74-543

This flax comb, set on a stand with turned legs, was probably used for finer counts (weights) of yarn than the previous model. The maker, time and exact location are unknown, but it is probably Mennonite.

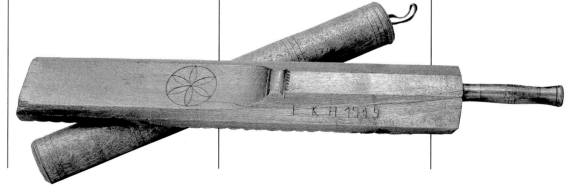

Food Gathering & Preparation

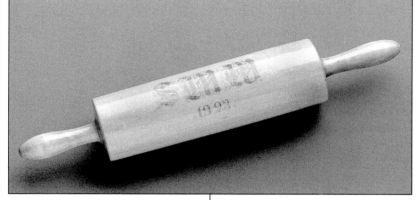

BEEHIVE
Reinhold D. Mallon
Poltimore, Quebec
ca. 1880
Wood, wheat straw
46 x 43 cm

CCFCS 84-176.1-2

Reinhold Mallon, who emigrated from Germany, made this dome-shaped hive (skep) for the Cheslock family in Poltimore. The technique of making baskets from coiled straw tied with elm bark is widespread in central Europe. Around 1905, wooden hives were adopted because retrieving the honey from straw skeps meant killing the bees every fall.

ROLLING PIN
Poplar Point, Manitoba
1923
Wood
44 x 7.5 cm (diam.)

CCFCS 77-435

This Hutterite rolling pin, finished in clear lacquer, bears the printed initials "S.M.W." and date "1923." This important tool for home baking was often given as a betrothal present by the groom-to-be.

DUCK DECOYS
Robert Romhild,
High Falls, Quebec
1935–1945

Robert Romhild was born in Ottawa in 1890 and worked as a mica miner at High Falls. He carved these decoys for his own use and painted them black, white, brown and red.

33 x 16 x 13 cm
CCFCS 84-110

29 x 14 x 9.3 cm
CCFCS 84-116

31 x 13 x 10 cm
CCFCS 84-117

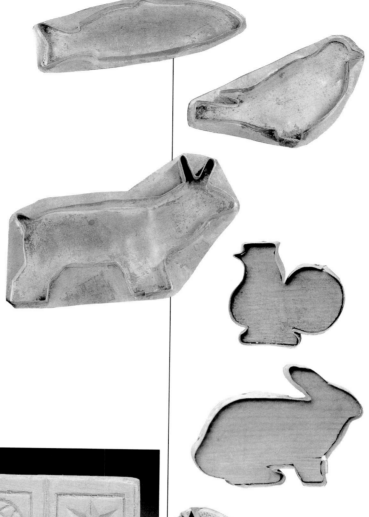

MENNONITE COOKIE CUTTERS
Saskatchewan
Wood, tin

These cookie cutters are tin silhouettes mounted on a wooden or metal base.

FISH
10 x 3.5 cm
CCFCS 75-1339

BIRD
9 x 4.5 cm
CCFCS 75-1341

DEER
11.5 x 8 cm
CCFCS 75-1335

CHICKEN
6.5 x 6.5 x 2 cm
CCFCS 78-622

RABBIT
10 x 7.5 x 2 cm
CCFCS 78-618

HORSE
11 x 11 x 7 cm
CCFCS 71-231

This cookie cutter with extra-large handgrip was made by Jacob Neudorf.

BIRD
8.5 x 6.5 x 2 cm
CCFCS 78-612

HORSE
7.5 x 7.5 x 2 cm
CCFCS 78-621

PASTRY PRINT
German
Dunnville, Ontario
Wood
23 x 17.8 cm
CCFCS 77-442

This pastry print was used to make fancy *Springerle* cookies, a Mennonite Christmas delicacy. The rectangular piece of wood is scored in twelve sections, each with a different incised design. Dough is placed over the pastry print, rolled to obtain imprints of the designs, then cut and baked.

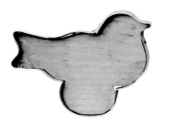

ROLLING PIN
Alberta
1944
Wood
46 x 7.3 cm (diam.)

CCFCS 81-142

This Hutterite rolling pin is made of one piece of wood but has a clear finish on the main part and a dark finish on the handles. It bears the inscription "Marie Waldner" and the date "1944," and is painted with black and red flowers.

SKIMMER
Erbsville, Waterloo, Ontario
Wood, iron, brass
122 x 22 cm

CCFCS 77-148

Skimmers are used to remove solids that rise to the surface during boiling. This model was either a lard or maple-sugar skimmer. It has a wooden handle with a wrought-iron collar at the base. Riveted to a brass bowl with holes drilled through it, the wrought-iron stem bears the inscription "WM FRIT."

CABBAGE SLICER
Ottawa Valley(?)
Wood, metal
118 x 33 x 28 cm

CCFCS 92-138

The cabbage slicer was an important tool in making sauerkraut. This model has a board base fitted with an angled blade over which a box containing a head of cabbage can be slid back and forth to slice it. The sliced cabbage is then made into sauerkraut.

Pottery

*I*n nineteenth-century Ontario, various small potteries supplied the demand for inexpensive utility wares made from local clays. These potteries were often family enterprises, run as a part-time venture combined with farming. Many were founded by German or Pennsylvania German craftsmen.

JAR
Joseph Wagner
Berlin, Ontario
1869–1880
Earthenware
21.7 x 12 cm
HIS 980.111.94

This clear-glazed jar, used to preserve tomatoes or fruit, bears an impression of the maker's name. Joseph Wagner was the son of Anselm, who had emigrated from Alsace in the 1840s and founded the pottery in Berlin (Kitchener). Joseph's Berlin pieces are now rare, because the pottery closed in the 1880s and he moved to Stratford.

JUG
J.M. Marlatt
Paris, Ontario
Mid-nineteenth century
Stoneware
28.3 x 17 cm
HIS 980.111.141

This salt-glazed jug is decorated with a cobalt-blue flower and shows an impression of the maker's mark on the shoulder. Similar stylized flowers are still used as motifs on some Austrian pottery. Although both stoneware and earthenware are made from clay, stoneware has a higher content of flint or sand, making it hard and dense.

PIE PLATE
William Eby
Conestogo, Ontario
1855–1907
Earthenware
24 x 4.5 cm
HIS 980.111.214

This red-clay plate is coated with a clear glaze. Two pieces of fruit are painted in dark brown slip on the inside. Pie plates with this motif are attributed to William Eby, based on shards found during excavations at the site of his pottery. Eby was a second-generation Ontario Mennonite of Pennsylvania German descent.

Toys & Games

TWIN DOLLS
Waterloo County, Ontario
Early twentieth century
Cotton, wool, linen
42 x 22 cm

CCFCS 84-8 and 84-9

These identical dolls are made of white linen, oil-painted pink. Their outfits and braided hair show evidence of careful Mennonite craftsmanship.

TOY DOG
Waterloo County, Ontario
Early twentieth century
Cloth
22 x 18 cm

CCFCS 84-7

Made of brown commercial fabric, this toy dog has buttons for eyes and a strip of burgundy fabric for a collar. It was sewn by hand and machine by a Mennonite woman.

DOLL CRADLE
Hague area, Saskatchewan
1890–1901
Wood, metal, porcelain
53.5 x 46.1 x 31 cm

CCFCS 72-670

In many details, this beautifully made doll cradle is like a full-sized Mennonite baby cradle. Its dovetail corners are held together with nails, screws and glue. "Baby" is painted on the ends of the cradle, and multicoloured leaves and scrolls are painted on the rockers and upper part. On each side are two porcelain knobs. On the top-end boards are holes which can be used for carrying the cradle. The maker is not known.

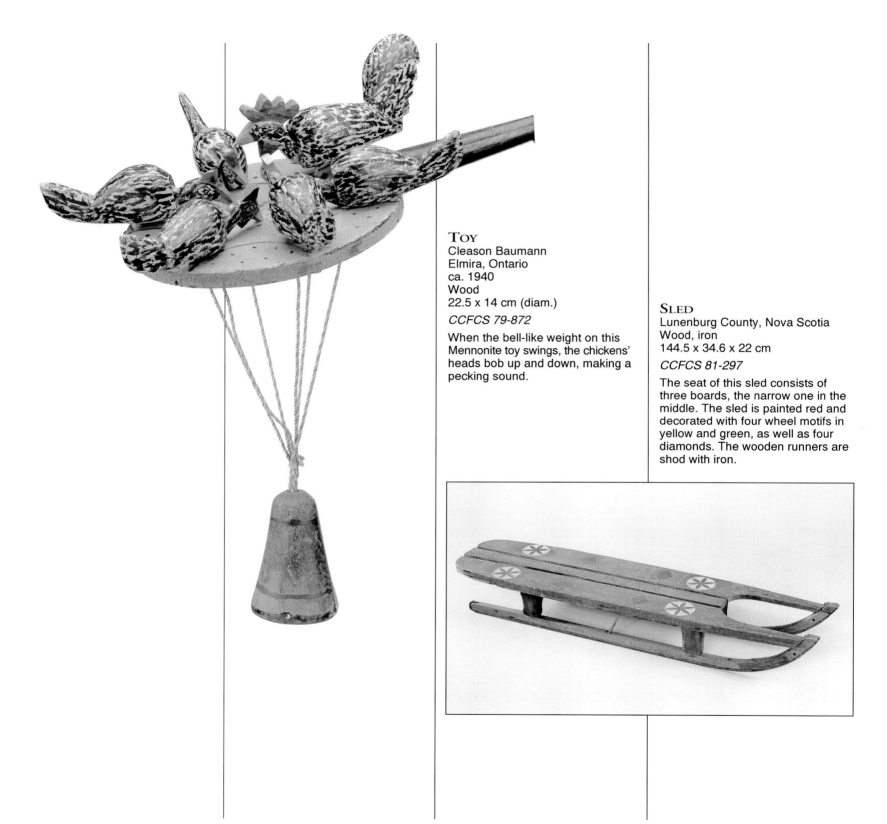

TOY
Cleason Baumann
Elmira, Ontario
ca. 1940
Wood
22.5 x 14 cm (diam.)
CCFCS 79-872

When the bell-like weight on this Mennonite toy swings, the chickens' heads bob up and down, making a pecking sound.

SLED
Lunenburg County, Nova Scotia
Wood, iron
144.5 x 34.6 x 22 cm
CCFCS 81-297

The seat of this sled consists of three boards, the narrow one in the middle. The sled is painted red and decorated with four wheel motifs in yellow and green, as well as four diamonds. The wooden runners are shod with iron.

ROCKING HORSE

Jake Wollman
Leask Colony, Saskatchewan
1963
Wood, iron
92.5 x 63 x 18.5 cm

CCFCS 77-825

Instead of making the familiar rocking horse, Hutterite carpenter Jake Wollman devised this toy horse for swinging the rider back and forth. The horse is suspended from the frame by two iron rods, which run through holes in the wooden bars at the horse's feet and are bent and hinged to the frame.

CHILDREN'S WAGON

Jacob Wipf
Magrath, Alberta
1959
Wood, metal
66 x 35.6 x 25.4 cm

CCFCS 71-187

This play wagon with just two wheels and an extra-long handle is used by older children to pull younger siblings around the Hutterites' housing compound. The long handle invites several children to pull, encouraging cooperative effort.

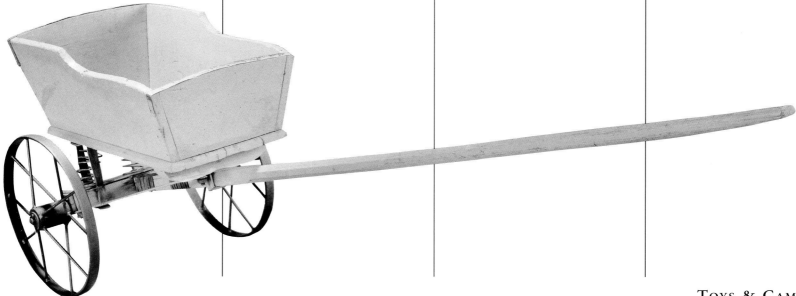

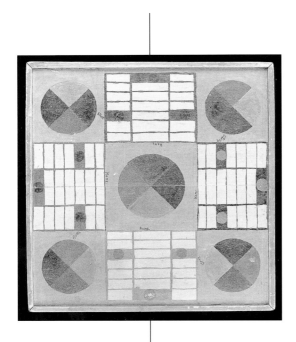

DOUBLE GAMEBOARD
Robert Romhild
High Falls, Quebec
Early 1900s
Wood
54.7 x 52.7 x 4 cm

CCFCS 84-109

In Canada, gameboards were often handmade and decorated in different folk-art styles. One side of this double gameboard is for chequers, the other for parcheesi. The board was a gift for Robert Romhild's relative Richard Thom, of German Road, Poltimore, Quebec.

GAMEBOARD
Nova Scotia
1800–1825
Wood
42.2 x 35.8 cm

CCFCS 81-8

On one side this board is elaborately carved with a compass-drawn star and four hearts, and on the reverse shows chequerboard markings. This item was found during renovations in a house owned by a sea captain in the early 1800s.

Musical Instruments

DULCIMER
Hardwood, metal
114.5 x 38 x 12 cm

CCFCS 84-404

The dulcimer's music is produced by striking the strings with a wooden hammer. This model, used by a family whose ancestors migrated from Germany around 1850, is relatively common among German households in Waterloo County.

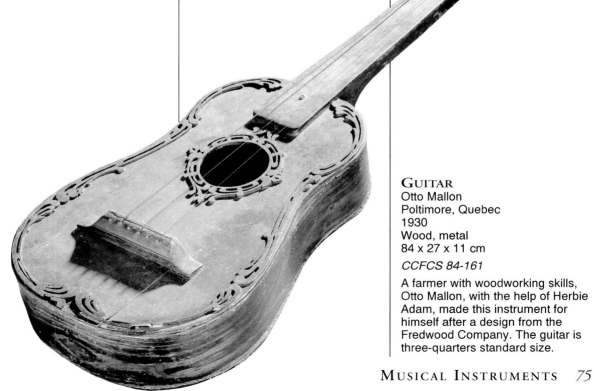

GUITAR
Otto Mallon
Poltimore, Quebec
1930
Wood, metal
84 x 27 x 11 cm

CCFCS 84-161

A farmer with woodworking skills, Otto Mallon, with the help of Herbie Adam, made this instrument for himself after a design from the Fredwood Company. The guitar is three-quarters standard size.

Fraktur & Imagery

The name Fraktur, referring to both writing and illumination, is derived from the medieval writing style that appears to be broken, or fractured. Eventually, the illustrations around the text became more prominent—in some cases, as in Anna Nance Weber's work, replacing the text altogether. The tradition of manuscript illumination was brought from Switzerland and southern Germany to Pennsylvania and from there to southern Ontario.

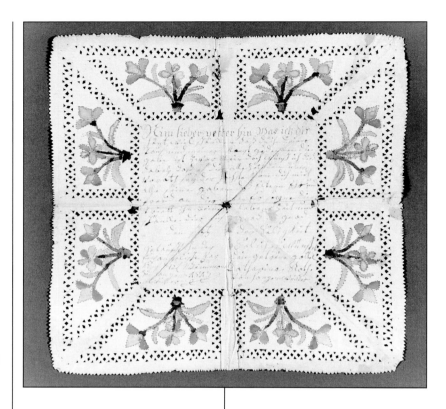

CERTIFICATE
Port Colborne, Niagara, Ontario
1812
Paper, wood, glass
34 x 33.7 cm
CCFCS 82-202

This paper cutout decorated with bouquets, serrated edges and pin-holes records the birth of Catherina Rolf in 1812. The wooden frame is painted gold.

FRAKTUR CERTIFICATE
Vaughan, Ontario
1810
Paper
58.5 x 48.2 cm
CCFCS 76-481

This is the birth and baptismal certificate of Daniel Hanauer, born in 1800 in Somerset County, Pennsylvania. The certificate is dated 1810. The Fraktur-style writing is surrounded by multicoloured birds, flowers and compass stars. The symmetrical arrangement of the decorative elements is characteristic of early Pennsylvania German folk art. Vaughan, where this Fraktur was probably finished, was settled around 1804 by Pennsylvanians from Somerset County.

FRAKTUR INSCRIPTION
Mennon, Saskatchewan
1882
Paper, wood, glass
52 x 20 cm
CCFCS 82-198

This Russian Mennonite inscription decorated with floral motifs and written in green, yellow and purple says "In your youth you should work diligently, because once you're old work will seem harder."

LEAVES FROM A NOTEBOOK
Ontario
Early nineteenth century
Watercolour on paper

These watercolours in the style of Pennsylvania German Fraktur seem to be pages from a book: they have dark stains along the top, right and bottom edges, but the left edge is clean. They are said to be from the Hauser family, which emigrated from Pennsylvania around 1800.

HEART AND FLOWERS
29.7 x 20.3 cm
CCFCS 79-1578

FLOWERS
29.9 x 20.4 cm
CCFCS 79-1577

BIRDS AND FLOWERS
29.9 x 20.6 cm
CCFCS 79-1576

PICTURE
Anna Nance Weber
Waterloo County, Ontario
1881
Watercolour on paper
23 x 19 cm

CCFCS 78-266

Anna Weber was born in Lancaster County, Pennsylvania, and immigrated to Canada in 1825. She did most of her drawings and paintings during the 1870s and 1880s (see biographical sketch). This painting of two blue horses is signed "Anna Weber hat das gemacht den 8 Februar 1881." (Anna Weber made this on February 8, 1881.)

PICTURE
Anna Nance Weber
Waterloo County, Ontario
1874
Watercolour on paper
18.4 x 11.4 cm

CCFCS 78-552

This Fraktur of floral motifs and birds symmetrically arranged inside a border is one example of illustration replacing text altogether.

Embroidery

SAMPLER
Alberta
1917
Linen, cotton
48.2 x 48.2 cm

CCFCS 73-1

Samplers were the work of young girls practising the art of embroidery for towels, pictures, kerchiefs and so on. They also preserved the tradition of different stitches, designs and motifs from one generation to the next. Samplers are usually signed and dated.

The fine needlework on this linen Hutterite sampler features multi-coloured letters, numerals, birds, geometric figures and a human.

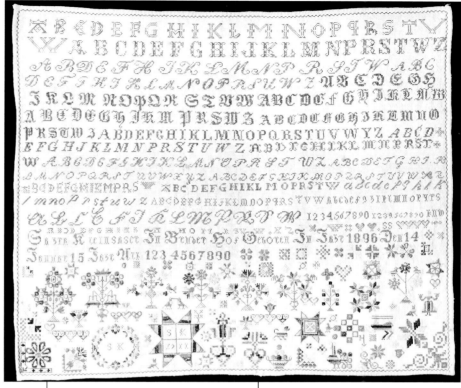

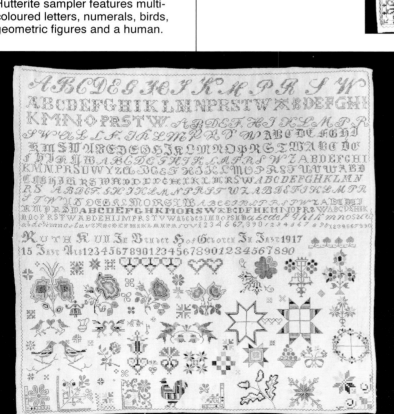

SAMPLER
Sadie Kleinsasser
1896
Linen, cotton
41.9 x 36.8 cm

CCFCS 73-2

Sadie Kleinsasser was fifteen when she embroidered this panel. It was brought to Canada in 1911 when many Hutterites from the northern United States began to migrate to Canada.

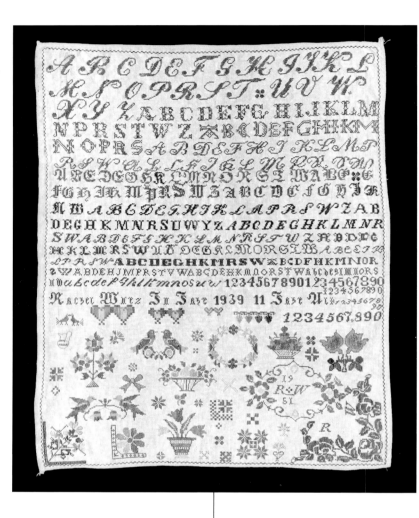

SAMPLER
Rachel Wutz
Alberta
1939
Linen, cotton
52.1 x 40.6 cm

CCFCS 73-3

Rachel Wutz was only eleven when she created this very fine embroidery of multicoloured cotton thread on linen.

SAMPLER
Katharina Wipf
Magrath, Alberta
1909
Linen, cotton
46 x 41.5 cm

CCFCS 71-202

Born in 1894, Katharina Wipf was fifteen when she made this sampler. Dated and initialled, it shows the alphabet and numbers as well as folk-art motifs. The informal composition of the folk-art motifs on the bottom third contrast with the more rigid lines of the various letters.

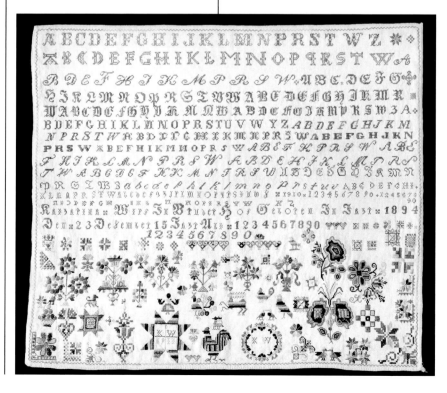

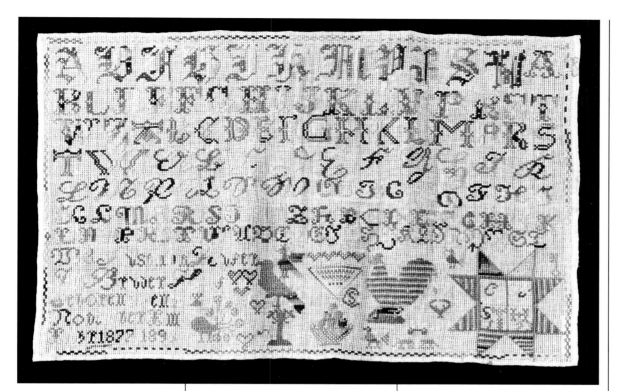

SAMPLER
Justina Hofer
Saskatchewan
1830s
Linen, wool
65 x 40 cm

CCFCS 77-855

This large Hutterite sampler is embroidered with letters, bird and star motifs in multicoloured wool thread.

SAMPLER
Poplar Point, Manitoba
Twentieth century
Linen, cotton
56 x 49 cm

CCFCS 77-430

This panel of unbleached linen is embroidered in multicoloured cotton. The alphabet on the top portion is finished, but the bottom, decorated with flowers, birds and butterflies, is unfinished.

SAMPLER
Anna Wipf
Saskatchewan
1921
Linen, cotton
150 x 40 cm
CCFCS 78-233

This commercial dish towel of white linen with a vertical red border was embroidered by hand with multi-coloured cotton thread and inscribed "Anna born in 1908, November 23." In the right-hand corner is the date: 1921.

SAMPLER
Rebecca Hofer
Saskatchewan
ca. 1930
Linen, cotton
72 x 42 cm
CCFCS 78-235

This commercial white linen towel displays a variety of colourful embroidered patterns. In German, the artist has embroidered "Rebecca Hofer, born April 6, 1917."

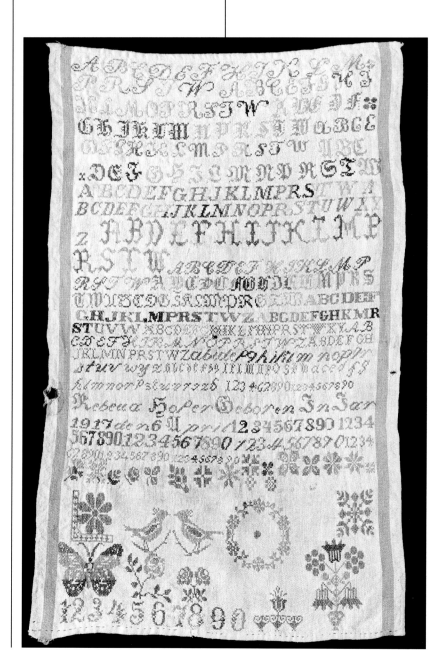

SAMPLER
Margaret Gross
Saskatchewan
1958
Linen, cotton
68 x 40 cm

CCFCS 78-240

Another commercial white linen dish towel with a vertical red-and-blue border is richly embroidered with various motifs. Dated 1958, the towel is embroidered with the phrase " Born in Year 1945   May 3 Margaret Gross."

SAMPLER
Saskatchewan
1933
Linen, cotton
176 x 36 cm

CCFCS 78-419

The simple embroidery on this linen towel consists of the alphabet and a centred, eight-corner star with the initials "E.H." and the date "1933."

RIBBON KEEPSAKE
1851
Cotton, wool, cardboard
31 x 7 cm
CCFCS 78-214

This type of Hutterite ribbon keepsake was also known as a mourning sampler. Pink-and-black striped ribbon is attached to an embroidered piece of cardboard. The embroidery, in black thread, reads "Alfred Risser Died November 17 1851, Aged 18. Prepare to meet thy God. They rest from their labours and their works. Do follow them LR." In the centre of the cardboard, a small opening reveals a miniature braid of hair, framed by a floral motif cross-stitched in red wool. The name Risser (Reeser, Reesor, Rissor) is a Bernese Anabaptist family name.

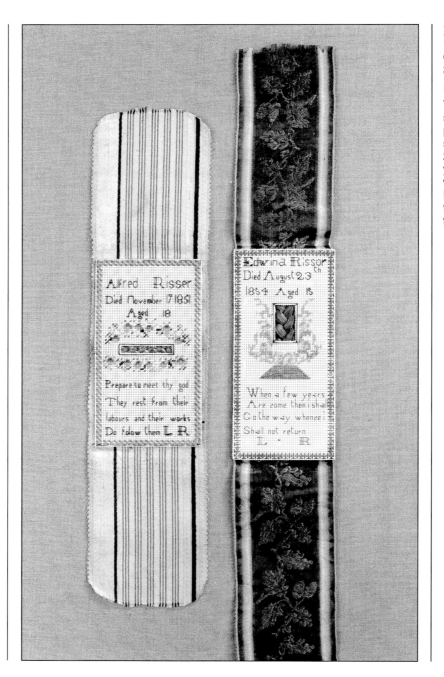

RIBBON KEEPSAKE
1854
Cardboard, cotton, silk
38 x 6 cm
CCFCS 78-215

The ribbon on this Hutterite keepsake is in a black-and-red oak leaf pattern, and the script is much the same: "Edwina Rissor Died August 23 1854 aged 15 When a Few years Are come then i shall Go the way Whence i shall not return LR" Roses in a vase are embroidered in the centre, and a small opening frames a tiny braid of hair.

Knick-knacks

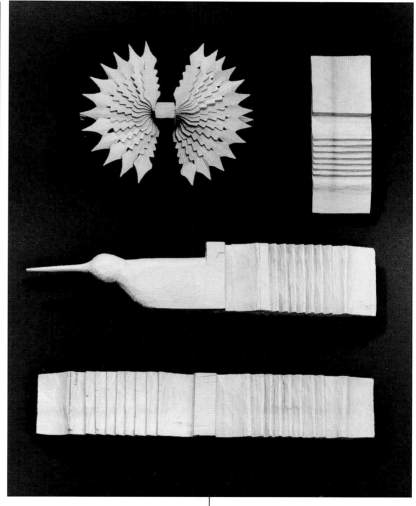

FAN-BIRD AND SECTIONS
Mr. and Mrs. Dave Isaacs
(see biographical sketch)
Osler, Saskatchewan
Wood
Parts 1 to 3, body, tail, wings, crest:
28 x 18 cm
Part 4, body, beak, tail: 35 x 7 cm
Part 5, wing: 33 x 6.3 cm
Part 6, crown for head: 17.5 x 6 cm
Part 7, wings: 17 x 15 x 5 cm

CCFCS 72-691.1-7

Fan-bird carving is found widely in Europe, from Scandinavia to Ukraine and Russia. Immigrants brought this carving tradition with them to Canada. The separately carved pieces pictured here show the process of fan-bird carving. All pieces were carved from lightweight wood. First, a block of wood is shaped to the desired span. The individual feathers are then split just to the base. After the wood is steamed, the feathers are twisted into position: the fan shape of the tail, wing or crest.

MODEL CHURCH
Adam Fuhr
Tavistock, Ontario
1910–1930
Wood, glass, metal
55.5 x 31.5 x 25.5 cm

CCFCS 84-102

Adam Fuhr, a cabinetmaker, gave this model to Reinhold Mallon, of Poltimore, in the 1930s. The "little church," with its glass windows and bell tower with metal cross, was used as a Christmas decoration. A small light inside the church gives off a warm glow through the golden glass windows.

Collins Eisenhauer

(1898–1979)   Lunenburg, Nova Scotia
(see biographical sketch)

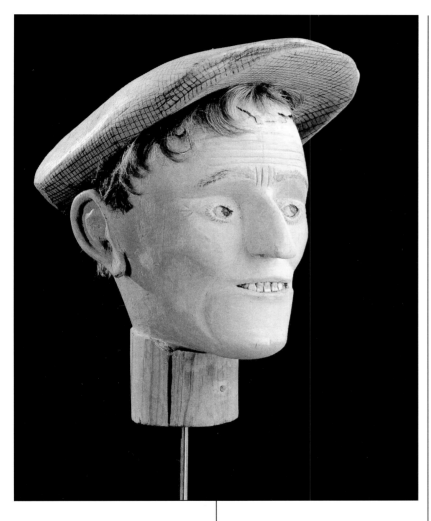

MAN'S HEAD
1976
Wood, metal, hair
43 x 24 x 16.5 cm

CCFCS 77-325

Collins Eisenhauer is believed to have started this head as a self-portrait but then changed it to someone anonymous. It does have some of Eisenhauer's features. Carved from one piece (except for the ears), the head wears a wooden cap with a chequered design added in pen. Real hair has been glued on, and the open mouth shows seven upper teeth: two white, five copper.

WOMAN FEEDING SKUNK
1965–1975
Wood
34.5 x 19.5 x 17.5 cm

CCFCS 77-286

In this carving, a nude, black-haired woman squats to feed a skunk. The figures are nailed to a green board, and the base is signed by the artist.

ROOSTER
1975
Wood, metal
44 x 37 x 13.5 cm

CCFCS 77-385

This carved black rooster with white spots has a red crop, yellow beak and brown metal legs.

CAT IN BOOT
1965–1975
Wood, bootlace
41 x 28 x 17 cm

CCFCS 77-288

A real bootlace is laced through this carving of a black and white cat in a large brown boot.

David Horst

(1873–1965) Waterloo, Ontario
(see biographical sketch)

Davidd Horst often reduced the third dimension of his work to the thickness of a board, while dealing with the other two dimensions in great detail.

RABBIT
1930–1939
Wood
7.3 x 7.2 x 3.3 cm
CCFCS 78-583

This rabbit is unpainted except for some tinting around its ears, eyes, mouth and paws. It has been mounted on a base carved with curved legs and decorated with dots.

COW
1930–1939
Wood
9.5 x 7.5 x 2.2 cm
CCFCS 78-584

This cow stands on an elaborately carved base with dark spots and lines.

CHICKEN
1930–1939
Wood, metal
9.2 x 6.8 x 2.3 cm
CCFCS 78-585

This green and blue speckled chicken with wire legs stands on a wooden base.

ROOSTER
1930–1939
Wood, metal
10.5 x 7.3 x 2.4 cm
CCFCS 78-586

Unpainted except for its head, this rooster stands on a base decorated with coloured spots.

Albert Lohnes

(1960–1975)   West Berlin, Nova Scotia
(see biographical sketch)

COVERED CHAIR
Wood, yarn
93.5 x 51 x 45.5 cm
CCFCS 77-304

Albert Lohnes, who went to sea at the age of thirteen, learned knotting or looping while working as a net-maker in seaside Nova Scotia. He made a covered chair when he heard his captain complain about sliding around in his chair in rough weather. Years later, after retire-ment, he began to make chair cov-ers again. This chair is completely covered with knotting. The white, black and red schooner on the seat sails on a blue background.

Jacob Neudorf

(?–1968) Neuhorst, Saskatchewan
(see biographical sketch)

A Mennonite, Jacob Neudorf carved for most of his life. Some changes in colouring and highlighting were done by Paul Lepp, the original collector.

WAPITI (AMERICAN ELK)
1960–1969
Wood
24.2 x 23.5 x 10.5 cm
CCFCS 74-454

The ears on this female wapiti are extended attentively.

MOUNTAIN SHEEP
1964–1968
Wood
25.6 x 20.5 x 12 cm
CCFCS 74-430

In this carving mounted on an oval board, the animal has turned its head slightly, as if alert to a nearby sound.

MOOSE
1960–1969
Wood
23 x 18.5 x 9 cm

CCFCS 74-455

A sense of heavyness is conveyed by this bull moose with long face, overhanging muzzle and palmate antlers.

STEER
1960–1969
Wood, glass
38 x 26 x 14 cm

CCFCS 74-320

This steer was carved from a single piece of wood, except for the horns, ears and genitals, which were glued on. The eyes are made of glass. Paul Lepp painted the ears, tail and hooves.

PONY
1964–1968
Wood
27 x 26.5 x 12.1 cm
CCFCS 74-437
More stylized than the previous carvings, this sandy-coloured pony with lowered head has light legs and belly, and dark tail and hooves.

HORSE
1964–1968
Wood
25.5 x 24 x 9 cm
CCFCS 74-431
This walking horse has grey spots, a dark brown mane and a sandy tail. The ears were carved separately.

HORSE
1964–1968
Wood
26 x 24.5 x 9 cm
CCFCS 74-424
Also in a walking stance, this horse has been stained a sandy colour, except for the black-painted hooves.

ROOSTER
1964–1968
Wood
22 x 19 x 5.5 cm
CCFCS 74-456

This brightly painted rooster is shown in a running position.

COW
1960–1969
Wood, glass
31 x 24.5 x 10 cm
CCFCS 74-321

This free-standing sculpture was carved from one piece except for the tail, ears, horns, udder and glass eyes. The hooves and tail are stained dark.

Henry B. Pauls

(1908–) Southern Ontario
(see biographical sketch)

Henry Pauls' paintings reveal a great love for detail, with trees, buildings, figures, waterways and meadows all telling stories of the past. A nostalgic mood permeates every scene. These paintings fall into two categories: those depicting life and landscapes from his native Russia; and those portraying his new home in Canada.

HIGHSCHOOL DAYS IN RUSSIA
1981
Oil on canvas board
30.5 x 25.3 cm
CCFCS 84-84

A girl and two boys in their school uniforms walk along a country road. Donated by the artist.

FERRY ON THE DNIEPR
1976
Oil on masonite
60.5 x 41 cm

CCFCS 84-77

The ferry carrying two haywagons approaches the shore, while the river flows toward the background. Donated by the artist.

MENNONITE FARMSTEAD IN RUSSIA
Oil on canvas board
50.8 x 40.5 cm

CCFCS 84-74

Several people work busily in the yard of this Russian farmhouse. On one side is an outdoor oven. Bake ovens were built outside to avoid excessive heat in the summer and the danger of fire. Donated by the artist.

MENNONITE KITCHEN IN RUSSIA
1984
Oil on canvas board
50.8 x 40.5 cm

CCFCS 84-73

This large room with a ladder leading upstairs is typical of Mennonite homes in Ukraine. Donated by the artist.

BLESSING THE BREAD
1984
Oil on canvas board
102 x 61.5 cm

CCFCS 84-80

In the centre of a small meadow surrounded by trees, a family gathers around a table, about to bless the freshly baked bread. Off to one side is the oven. Donated by the artist.

FARM IN SASKATCHEWAN
1979
Oil on masonite
75.5 x 48 cm

CCFCS 84-81

This was the home of the Bernhard Pauls family from 1926 to 1931. The person on horseback is preparing to bring in the cows. Donated by the artist.

WATERMELON SYRUP COOKING
1984
Oil on canvas
132.5 x 76.8 cm

CCFCS 84-82

While some people cook the sweet liquid from a watermelon into a syrup, others play and eat. (For more information on watermelons in the Mennonite diet, see the article by Steve Prystupa in this volume.)

HE WHO PLANTS A GARDEN ...
Oil on plywood
52.7 x 40.5 cm

CCFCS 84-451

A man works in his garden near the blossoming boughs of a tree. His kneeling posture is appropriate to the sentiment: "He who plants a garden works hand in hand with God." (For more information on this painting and the next, see the article by Robert Klymasz in this volume.)

KNEELING IN A GARDEN
Oil on plywood
51 x 40.62 cm

CCFCS 84-452

This illustrated poem takes the sentiment of the previous painting several steps further. The physical aspects of gardening become metaphors for moral values: sowing the seeds of forgiveness; burying anger and resentment; digging down to true understanding.

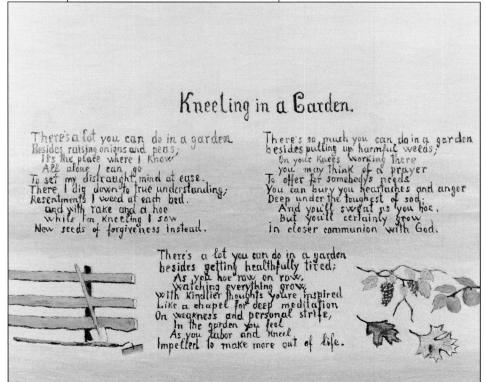

Ewald Rentz

(1908–   ) Beardmore, Ontario
(see biographical sketch)

On his travels through the bush as a prospector, Ewald Rentz collects branches and roots of interesting shapes. He says he does not create art—he just "completes" what he brings home.

BELLHOP
ca. 1975
Wood, metal, glass
49 x 31 x 16 cm
CCFCS 80-118

The exaggerated stride of this glass-eyed bellhop-monkey is presumably aimed at fulfilling the promises printed on the suitcases: "We are on time" and "We are never late."

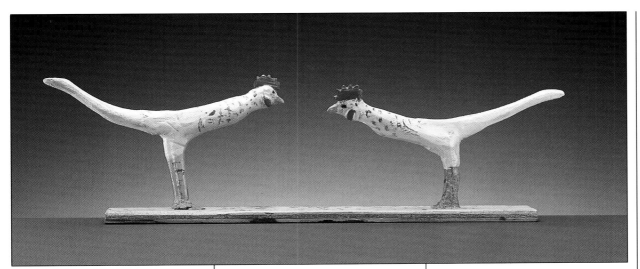

COCKFIGHT
1975
Wood
41.3 x 12.5 x 5 cm
CCFCS 80-117

Two white and reddish-brown roosters confront each other in an aggressive posture.

TURKEY
ca. 1975
Wood, leather, fungi
92 x 51 x 35 cm
CCFCS 80-115

A tree burl forms the body of this turkey, while the tail is made of fan-fungus. Smaller fungi nailed to the neck suggest the fleshy lobe pendant of the wattle.

Jacob Roth

(1896–   ) Ailsa Craig, Ontario
(see biographical sketch)

Jacob Roth was born in Punkeydoodles Corners, Waterloo, Ontario. He began making miniatures and models in his eighty-second year "for the health and for the pastime." His works chronicle familiar scenes from Mennonite farm life.

COVERED WAGON
Wood, metal, cloth
71.2 x 29.4 x 22.5 cm
CCFCS 90-10

This miniature covered wagon, drawn by two reddish-brown horses with black wool manes and tails, carries four men and two women wearing Mennonite cloth garb and wooden hats. The wagon is not in the characteristic boat shape of the famous Conestoga wagons.

CATTLE AUCTION
Wood, metal, cloth
66.1 x 30.7 x 17.8 cm
CCFCS 90-7

Several men are gathered before the auctioneer, who points a stick in the direction of a potential buyer.

NEW HAMBURG
FIRE WAGON
Wood, metal, cloth, vinyl
103.9 x 31 x 20.4 cm

CCFCS 90-8.1-2

Fascinated by the New Hamburg fire department's horse-drawn wagon, Jacob Roth constructed this model in its honour. The wagon itself is made of tin; the wooden horses have black wool manes and tails; the firefighters' clothing is of vinyl; and plastic tubes serve as fire hoses.

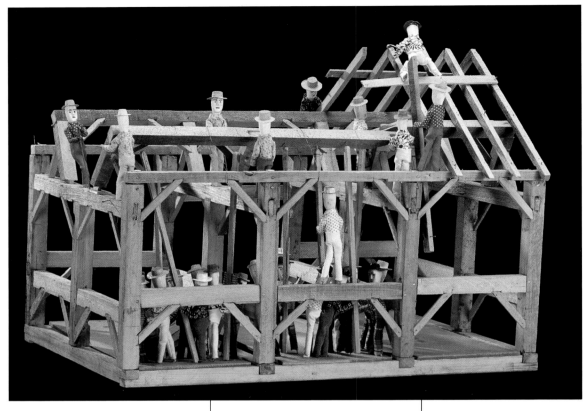

BARN RAISING
Wood, metal, cloth
77.5 x 64.7 x 51 cm

CCFCS 90-4

Directed by a foreman, twenty-two men position one of the main beams for the roof of a new barn. Five other men frame the roof on one end (see detail on right). This model accurately conveys the cooperative effort of barn raising, a custom among Mennonites in Waterloo County for many generations.

QUILTING BEE
Wood, metal, cloth
31 x 22.4 x 16.5 cm
CCFCS 90-6

Chequered material covers the base of this diorama of twelve women sitting around a quilting frame. Each woman works with her right hand, resting the left hand in her lap.

MILKING THE COWS
35.7 x 30.4 x 13 cm
CCFCS 90-3

In this playful diorama, three cats gather in anticipation of milk that may be spilt when the women milk their Holsteins.

Biographical Sketches

AUGUST BOEHME (1841–1907)

August Boehme and his wife, Mary Kielow, emigrated from Brandenburg to the Ottawa Valley in 1865. Although a blacksmith by trade, he was also a skilled woodworker. He worked in several townships in Renfrew County, staying with different families while making their furniture. In 1874 he applied for a Crown grant of 200 acres in Raglan Township and gave up carpentry as his main occupation. In the 1881 census, he was listed as a farmer, thirty-nine, with his wife Mary, twenty-nine, and seven children born in Ontario.

The Boehme farm was isolated, nearly three kilometres from the nearest neighbour. At first, they lived in a shanty, but Boehme soon built his family a two-storey log house, still largely intact. He also built the furniture, some of which is still used by his grandson Oscar. Besides working in pine, Boehme often chose black ash for his work. Because of the poor soil and harsh environment of Boehme's farm, the ash grew slowly, thereby producing a lot of heartwood.

In 1905, Boehme transferred his farm to his son and daughter-in-law and moved to a small retirement home he had built on the land for himself and his second wife. He died there in 1907.

Boehme is known mostly for his cupboards, some of which are illustrated in books of early Canadian furniture. His style is described as "displaying folk-craft tradition owing nothing to the style books" (Phillip Shackleton, *The Furniture of Old Ontario*) and "a reflection of a common form in the German rural tradition" (Howard Pain, *The Heritage of Upper Canadian Furniture*). The chair on page 47 is a good example of the latter statement.

Although Boehme did not sign his pieces, he wrote the name of the customer and the completion date in German script on the inside of the top left door of his cupboards. These markings, together with his distinctive scrolled pediments, make identification relatively certain.

COLLINS EISENHAUER (1898–1979)

Collins Eisenhauer was born at Scarsdale, Lunenburg County, Nova Scotia, in 1898, one of a family of seven brothers and seven sisters. His father was a stonemason who built his own house. Eisenhauer's great-grandparents had come from Germany.

As a child, Eisenhauer dreamed of being a painter, but family circumstances required him to leave school after grade three. He took any job he could find, beginning with apple picking and later working at logging and farming and in the tobacco fields of Ontario. His farthest trips were to Manitoba by train and to Barbados on a trading vessel out of Lunenburg.

When he retired, Eisenhauer felt it was too late to learn painting; instead, in 1964, he started carving. He placed his first carving, a swan, in his yard. Five more swans, and then other sculptures, followed. He gave some pieces away and sold several others for very little money. When some of his works were exhibited at the Bowmanville Antiques and Folk Art Show in 1974, Eisenhauer achieved wider recognition as a folk artist.

Eisenhauer specialized in life-sized carvings of people and animals. Perhaps his most famous carvings are those of four politicians: Pierre Elliott Trudeau, Robert Stanfield, David Lewis and Gerald Regan. Eisenhauer spent a whole year preparing these sculptures for a parade in New Germany, Nova Scotia, in 1974.

Eisenhauer also produced a number of miniatures, inspired by his own mischievous and erotic sense of humour. He liked to portray unorthodox relationships between humans and animals, as in *Woman Feeding Skunk* (page 87) and *Accordion Player and Dancing Animals*.

The CCFCS collection contains a number of excellent examples of Eisenhauer's work.

DAVID B. HORST (1873–1965)

David Horst of St. Jacobs, Waterloo County, Ontario, was a member of the Old Order Mennonite community. In his youth he travelled as far as Michigan and Florida on different business ventures, but returned to his native community when they proved unsuccessful. Horst started carving seriously only after becoming partially paralysed by a stroke in 1935. He created numerous small animal carvings, most of which he gave to family, friends and members of the community in gratitude for looking after him. Visitors often asked for one of the delicate carvings to take home as a memento and left a small remuneration in return.

In his work Horst used mostly basswood, which is easy to carve. He supported the piece with his lame hand while carving or painting with the other. Carving familiar animals, he showed ingenuity in his creation of expressive features and great concern even for minute details. Most pieces were finished with watercolours and set on simple bases made of scrap wood, ornamented with red and green spots. Horst broke from his tradition of animals when he carved a statue of King George V, who visited Canada in 1935. Relatives report that he kept a newspaper picture of the monarch on which to base his sculpture.

Only after his death was Horst's art recognized by a wider public. Now, he is appreciated as one of Ontario's outstanding woodcarvers in the Pennsylvania German tradition.

MR. AND MRS. DAVE ISAACS (WORKED PRE-1970)

Mr. and Mrs. Dave Isaacs lived near Osler, Saskatchewan, where together they worked in the art of bird carving. Originally, they painted their finely carved parts with watercolours. However, in their later work, they switched to enamel paints. By 1972 they had given up their craft because they felt they were too old.

ABRAHAM LATSCHAW (1799–1870)

Abraham Latschaw was born in Berks County, Pennsylvania, of Swiss-German parents. In 1822 he immigrated to Canada, where he lived near Mannheim, south of Berlin (Kitchener). His earliest work was the art of Fraktur, or German manuscript illumination. In one year he produced few but superb pieces of Fraktur, among them the flyleaves in Bishop Benjamin Eby's Bible, generally recognized as some of the most outstanding examples of Pennsylvania German Fraktur in Ontario.

In the 1830s he launched a cabinetmaking business, which continued into the 1860s. Over the years a number of people, including his father, Isaac, and a brother, Isaac Junior, worked in his shop at Mannheim to help with turning, painting and other tasks. However, Abraham seems to have been the dominant force of the enterprise. Many pieces from his workshop feature folk-art motifs like inlaid tulips, painted compass stars and trees.

Identifying Latschaw's pieces is difficult because he continually experimented with new ideas and styles during his thirty years in the business. Identification is now possible only by comparing an item with documented pieces of his work.

ALBERT LOHNES (1895–1977)

Albert Lohnes was born at Ragged Harbour, Lunenburg County, Nova Scotia, in 1895. When he was thirteen, he left home to sail with an American captain. Five years later a serious injury to his hand sent him to hospital, where doctors wanted to amputate. Lohnes refused, and his hand did eventually heal, although his fingers remained slightly stiff. After his hospital stay, Lohnes sailed out of Gloucester, Massachusetts, for many years.

When Lohnes was about thirty, he fashioned a chair cover out of different yarns, in response to a complaint by the ship's captain that he slid around on his chair during heavy storms. Lohnes had learned knotting while working on ship's nets.

Several years after retiring and moving home to Nova Scotia, he developed knee problems and decided to "knit chairs" to keep busy. He is known to have decorated at least sixteen chairs in Nova Scotia and may have done as many as twenty.

The chair shown on page 90 is a fine example of his craftsmanship.

JACOB NEUDORF (? —1968)

Jacob Neudorf, who lived first in and then near Osler, Saskatchewan, seems to have carved for most of his life. His miniature animals—both domestic and wild—are realistically styled, life-like in their characteristic positions. Some of his sculptures were later highlighted with paint by Paul Lepp of Saskatoon.

The Museum holds an excellent collection of Neudorf's carvings.

HENRY B. PAULS (1908—   )

Henry Pauls was born in the Mennonite settlement of Chortitza, Russia, in 1908. That same year his parents moved to the island of Chortitza, where his father bought a farm. In 1916 they were forced to sell, and moved to the nearby community of Rosenthal. The years 1916 to 1923 were very hard years in Russia, with war, epidemics and famine. During the Bolshevik revolution, the Mennonites were declared rich people and all their belongings were confiscated. Only help from American Mennonites saved them from starvation.

The Pauls managed to come to Canada in 1923. In 1937, Henry Pauls married Sara Hildebrand, who had been born in Einlage, Russia, and who had come to Canada in 1927. They made their home on a bush farm near Sonningdale, Saskatchewan, and later moved to southern Ontario.

In the 1970s Henry and Sara retired from tomato and vegetable farming, and Henry began to paint scenes from his Russian childhood and his farming days in Canada. Most of the paintings in the CMC collection were donated by Henry Pauls. They provide a fascinating record of Mennonite life in Russia and Canada.

EWALD RENTZ (1908–   )

Ewald Rentz was born in Wells, North Dakota. He had five brothers and three sisters. While he was still a boy his parents, who had been married in a Lutheran church in Winnipeg, returned to Manitoba to farm.

Rentz apprenticed as a barber in Winnipeg, then moved to Beardmore, Ontario. During World War II he worked in logging camps, and later he became a prospector in northern Ontario.

During his travels through the forests on prospecting trips, Rentz found unusually shaped pieces of wood, roots and fungi that inspired him. In his spare time at home, he worked with these natural objects to "free" their hidden shapes, turning them into sculptures. Rentz claimed that he never really created anything but coaxed out the form that was already there. He used plastic wood liberally, added limbs and finished his work with paint.

In April 1980, a collection of 145 sculptures by Rentz was shown at the Bowmanville Antiques and Folk Art Show and was later sold to a Toronto folk-art gallery. The CMC has acquired a number of his sculptures. Those shown in this volume are representative of his wide-ranging imagination, humour and inventiveness.

JACOB ROTH (1896–   )

Jacob Roth was born near Punkeydoodles Corners, Waterloo County, Ontario, and raised as a Mennonite. By the age of fourteen he was farming full-time with his father, but gained independence at age twenty-one by hiring himself out to other farmers. In 1920 he met his future wife, Melinda; after marrying, they bought a fifty-acre farm near Tavistock, Ontario, and began raising their family. Roth was a farmer most of his life, although his skill for mechanical work sometimes provided him with employment away from the farm.

After the hard years of the Depression, the Roths bought a 200-acre farm near Ailsa Craig, which they rehabilitated. Three years after Melinda died in 1968, Roth, then seventy-five, built a house in Tavistock with the help of his brother, David. At age eighty-two, he had to move in with his son Stanley.

This active craftsman, seemingly driven to continue working, built a workshop behind the house, where he started sculpting. His skilled hands created a special kind of multimedia folk art. Using wood, metal, fabric and plastic, he portrayed the scenes he witnessed throughout his life as a Mennonite farmer. Some of his best work was done in his eighties.

In fact, Roth continued to work on his assemblies and carvings into his nineties. He attributes his work on over 100 sculptures with keeping his mind and body healthy. His last sculptures were done in 1990.

The CMC purchased a number of sculptures by this skilled craftsman, who documented everyday scenes and local historical events from his long life in Waterloo County.

ANNA NANCE WEBER (1814–1888)

Born in 1814 in Lancaster County, Pennsylvania, Anna Weber immigrated to Ontario with her parents in 1825. They settled just north of Waterloo. Weber never married and apparently was an invalid for much of her life. In the 1870s and 1880s she produced a great number of very fine Fraktur watercolours. Although the art of Fraktur was on the wane by the 1850s, Weber carried the tradition well into the second half of the nineteenth century.

Weber's earliest dated and signed work is her own songbook, decorated in 1866. She made drawings upon request and probably also in gratitude to hosts. Her drawings, usually in blue, violet, ochre and green, often marked a special occasion like the birth of a friend's child. Her favourite motifs were stylized birds and plants, frequently arranged symmetrically.

Weber, who always signed and dated her work, was a prolific artist. She probably produced about 100 watercolour paintings in the Pennsylvania German folk-art tradition.

Bibliography

Archival material. CCFCS, 1970.

Bird, Michael. *Calligraphy to Cabinetmaking: The Fraktur and Furniture of Abraham Latschaw.* Kitchener: Schneider Haus.

———. *Canadian Folk Art: Old Ways in a New Land.* Toronto: Oxford University Press, 1983.

———. *Ontario Fraktur: A Pennsylvania-German Folk Tradition in Early Canada.* Toronto: M.F. Feheley Publishers, 1977.

———. "The Painted Furniture of John J. Gerber and Christian O. Gerber." *Waterloo Historical Society,* 69 (1981).

Bird, Michael, and Terry Kobayashi. *A Splendid Harvest: Germanic Folk and Decorative Arts in Canada.* Toronto: Van Nostrand Reinhold, 1981.

Flyer accompanying exhibition of J. Roth's sculptures. Kitchener: Schneider Haus, 1988.

Folk Art in Nova Scotia. Exhibition catalogue. Halifax: Art Gallery of Nova Scotia, 1976.

From the Heart: Folk Art in Canada. CCFCS exhibition catalogue. Toronto and Ottawa: McClelland and Stewart and National Museum of Man, 1983.

Patterson, Nancy-Lou Gellermann. *Swiss-German and Dutch-German Mennonite Traditional Art in the Waterloo Region, Ontario.* CCFCS Mercury Series No. 27. Ottawa: National Museum of Man, 1979.

Huntington, Chris. Interview with C. Eisenhauer, 1975. Chris Huntington Collection, HUN-A-3. Archives of the Canadian Centre for Folk Culture Studies (CCFCS).

Huntington, Chris, Personal communication, June 1991.

Kobayashi, Terry, and Michael Bird. *A Compendium of Canadian Folk Artists.* Erin, Ontario: Boston Mills Press, 1985.

Lee-Whiting, Brenda. *Harvest of Stones: The German Settlement in Renfrew County.* Toronto: University of Toronto Press, 1985.

———. *On Stony Ground.* Renfrew: Juniper Books, 1986.

Lepp, Wilbur. Letter to CCFCS, 1973. CCFCS Archives.

Mattie, Wesley. Taped interview with Ewald Rentz, 1980. CCFCS Archives.

Pain, Howard. *The Heritage of Upper Canadian Furniture.* Toronto: Van Nostrand Reinhold, 1978.

Pauls, Henry, and Sara Pauls. Manuscript of autobiographical sketches (English, German, Low German).

Roth, Stanley. Personal communication, June 1991.

A HISTORY OF GERMANS IN CANADA

HARTMUT FROESCHLE AND GEORG K. WEISSENBORN

IMMIGRATION IN THE EIGHTEENTH CENTURY

Although the presence of individual Germans in Canada had been documented long before, it was in September 1750 that German group immigration began with the arrival of the good ship *Ann* in Halifax harbour. The *Ann* carried about three hundred German passengers; they settled briefly in a part of Halifax that became known as German Town.

The British were then systematically recruiting "foreign" Protestants to populate the conquered territory of Acadia, trying to create a balance with the Roman Catholic French settlers already there. Recruitment in Europe was centralized in Rotterdam, Netherlands, in the hands of the merchant John Dick. Dick translated the official English recruiting pamphlet, *Historical and Geographical Description of Nova Scotia*, into German, rendering an inviting account of conditions in the new land. During the first three years of the recruiting policy, about two thousand Germans arrived in Nova Scotia, together with several thousand Irish and English immigrants. They had to earn their passage through hard work, building roads and fortifications.

At the end of May 1753, 1,453 Germans left their temporary huts within the fortress of Halifax and sailed southwest to Merliguesh Bay where, on June 7, they founded the town of Lueneburg (Lunenburg). This first German settlement in Canada initiated many more smaller ones in adjacent areas. The Nova Scotia census of 1766–67 showed 264 Germans among Halifax's 1,838 inhabitants, and 1,417 in Lunenburg where only 51 English people had settled.

In the mid-sixties, about one hundred Pennsylvania Germans arrived in the part of Nova Scotia that, in 1784, was severed and raised to the status of an independent province—New Brunswick. These immigrants, who had been recruited by a settlement agency, founded Germantown (now known as Shepody), Moncton and Coverdale.

The German settlers in Nova Scotia established the first Lutheran congregations in Canada, organized a school system and, by the end of the 1780s, had even initiated their own newspaper and almanac. When fellow countrymen began to arrive at the end of the American Revolution, this last influx revitalized the German element in Halifax.

When the American colonies rose against the motherland in 1775, Britain feared the loss of Canada. So when American troops laid siege to Quebec in 1776, an English relief army arrived under the command of General Burgoyne. Over four thousand of his troops were German auxiliaries sent by the principalities of Brunswick and Hessia; their commanding officer was General Friedrich Adolph von Riedesel.

At the end of the American Revolution in the early 1780s, many discharged German soldiers, about 2,400 in Canada, accepted Britain's generous offers to war veterans and remained in what was then British

North America. These colonists settled along the St. Lawrence River in the Province of Quebec and in the territory of the later Province of Upper Canada (Prince Edward County, Ontario), as well as in Nova Scotia (Annapolis County) and New Brunswick (at the lower St. John River). Most of the discharged German soldiers earned their keep as craftsmen and farmers.

Even more important than the discharged German and British troops were those who had remained true to the Crown throughout the war, the Empire Loyalists, who laid the foundation for Anglo-Canadian society. Among the forty-five thousand Loyalists who settled in the northern colonies after the war were a respectable number of Germans.

People of German origin had been just as divided as those of British background on the splitting of the colonies from the mother country. While Germans in other American colonies by and large supported the revolution eagerly, the situation in the Loyalist stronghold in New York State was different, for geographic and personal reasons. A considerable portion of the Palatines who had settled in the Hudson, Mohawk and Schoharie river valleys some eighty years earlier remained loyal to the Crown.

The pro-British position of the Germans on the Mohawk and Schoharie was due in no small part to the efforts of Sir John Johnson, a passionate Tory and the son of an Irish father and a German mother. Johnson succeeded in bringing the Mohawk Indians to the British side. Because they were far from political developments and did not want to be exposed to attack by the neighbouring Mohawks, many Germans in this region cast their lots with Britain. In 1776, Johnson fled to Canada, where he founded the 84th Royal New York Regiment. The "Royal Greens," composed largely of Sir John's German neighbours, made a name for themselves under Sir John's keen leadership.

As their property had been expropriated by the Americans, the members of this and other Loyalist regiments were granted land in Canada after the war. In Ontario alone, over one thousand German Loyalists and their families settled at the Bay of Quinte, along the St. Lawrence River and in the Niagara Peninsula; as well, German Loyalists established themselves in the Maritime provinces and in the southern portion of Quebec (on Missisquoi Bay, the northeastern point of Lake Champlain).

In the wake of the German auxiliary troops and the Loyalists came another group of German immigrants, a trickle at first that soon became a stream: the northward trek of Pennsylvania German farmers. William Penn had founded the State of Pennsylvania in the late seventeenth century as a haven for persecuted religious sects. In the course of the eighteenth century, Pennsylvania became home to a number of German Anabaptist religious communities, such as Mennonites and Amish, as well as Baptists

and Moravian (Herrnhut) Brethren, with the result of creating coherent German-speaking areas. These pioneer families had many children, and after two or three generations most of arable Pennsylvania was occupied. The Germans began to spread north, and in 1786 a number of German-speaking Mennonites and a small group of the Tunker sect (Baptists) arrived in Ontario.

The continuing influx of Pennsylvania German settlers led to the founding of a number of Mennonite congregations in Ontario, along with a Moravian congregation in Fairfield (a literal translation of the German name Schönfeld). The Fairfield group consisted largely of baptized Delaware Indians, led by the German-speaking missionary David Zeisberger.

In 1794, a group of 186 German immigrants (seventy-four households) arrived in Ontario. Coming from various parts of Germany, this group had been prepared, by a two-year sojourn in New York State, for residence in York County (Lake Ontario), a vast wilderness in which only a small British garrison had been stationed at Fort York. These new arrivals pioneered the founding of Toronto. Leading this well-equipped little band of farmers and artisans was William Berczy, born in Wallerstein, Germany, under the name of Johann Albrecht Ulrich Moll; this fascinating pioneer was not only a dynamic colonizer, but a gifted painter and architect as well. His group founded the town of Markham, north of Toronto.

IMMIGRATION IN THE NINETEENTH CENTURY

After the turn of the century the influx of Pennsylvania Germans assumed mass proportions. The longest-surviving German settlement, centred in Waterloo County on the Grand River, Ontario, started with a few settlers in 1799. In 1805 the "German Company," a Pennsylvania German land-development agency, acquired sixty thousand acres in the county. Waterloo and its neighbouring counties grew rapidly, for in addition to the flood of Pennsylvania Germans, it also attracted immigrants directly from Germany, starting in the 1820s. Many towns and villages were founded in Waterloo County, some of which still bear German names today: New Hamburg, Heidelberg, Breslau, Bamberg, Baden and others. In the mid-1830s, the name Berlin was adopted for the rapidly growing, German-speaking centre of the county; Mennonite elder Benjamin Eby suggested the name to acknowledge direct emigration from Germany and encourage its continued flow; in 1916, Berlin was renamed Kitchener.

Emigration from Germany (in particular southwest and western Germany) had increased in 1817 because of the economic crisis following the Wars of Liberation; in fact, 1817 and 1818 were record years for emigration. Poor potato and grain harvests in the mid-1840s prompted another record emigration from Germany, and after 1848, when the all-German parliament failed to create a united German state, Germans again left their homeland in record numbers. Canada attracted larger groups of these emigrants only in the mid-1830s.

Most of these immigrants went to southwestern Ontario; the Maritimes, owing to their remote location, had soon lost their attraction for immigrants. Montréal managed to lure several German artisans, so that by 1830 a German community began to exist there. It took another ten years for a German community to evolve in Toronto.

Between 1830 and 1870, emigrants from the interior of Germany swelled while Mennonite and other German-American migration dwindled. Two kinds of German farmers, craftsmen and workers migrated to southwestern Ontario: those who had chosen this area as their destination; and those who had originally planned to travel west but then shied away from the hardships of crossing the continent. By 1848, at least twelve thousand Germans from Germany proper—referred to as *Reichsdeutsche* (in contradistinction to the *Volksdeutsche* from German-speaking areas outside of Germany)—had arrived in southwestern Ontario. Of these, about nine thousand found a new home in Waterloo, more than one thousand went to the Niagara Peninsula and fifteen hundred settled in Perth and Huron counties.

Eastern Ontario had not attracted German settlers since the arrival of the Loyalists, but by the end of the 1850s arable land in southern Ontario was becoming scarce. Starting in 1857, the Canadian government's offers of free land for settlement lured German immigrants into the Ottawa Valley, where the sandy and stony soil was not very suitable for farming. By 1860, as many as ninety-five German families from Neumark, Pomerania and western Prussia (of whom about one-third were German-speaking Kaszuby from the Danzig district) had arrived in the Ottawa Valley. Between 1861 and 1870, another four thousand Germans made their home in the valley's Renfrew County. Also from 1861, both banks of the Ottawa River saw some other German settlements spring up simultaneously; they extended north of Buckingham (Labelle County) and Shawville (Pontiac County), with most of the settlers coming from eastern German territories.

German immigration into southeastern Ontario lasted until the beginning of the First World War. In the 1880s, western Canada started proving more attractive.

LATE NINETEENTH AND EARLY TWENTIETH CENTURY
While Canada's midwest remained practically devoid of immigrants until the 1870s, the far west experienced a brief population boom in the fifties. A number of German pioneers belonging to this group are known by name;

they were followed by many other individual immigrants. German group immigration to British Columbia is discernible only since the 1920s.

Mass migration to the Canadian West was systematically promoted through the Homesteading Act of 1872. In addition, land settlement agencies worked for the Canadian Pacific and Canadian National railway companies. From 1896, the Laurier government also pushed western immigration. Thus, it is hardly surprising that, together with large numbers of British, American, Ukrainian, Polish and Scandinavian immigrants, many German immigrants also went west. Significantly, a major portion of German-speaking immigrants did not come directly from Germany proper; between 1900 and 1910, only ten to fifteen per cent did so, while forty to forty-five per cent of German-speaking immigrants came from Russia (southern Ukraine, Volhynia, Volga area), approximately twenty-five per cent from Eastern Europe (Galicia, Bukowina, Banat, Dobrucha) and almost twenty per cent from the United States.

For decades, group settlement of the West by religious and ethnic criteria was an established pattern; in the case of the Germans, Mennonites dominated in Manitoba, Roman Catholics in Saskatchewan and Lutherans in Alberta. Almost seven thousand Mennonites from Ukraine settled in southern Manitoba between 1874 and 1879, even before the railways reached Winnipeg in 1882. In the so-called East Reserve and West Reserve they founded many towns: Steinbach, Gretna, Altona and Winkler are the best known today. Many of the original 110 settlements have been incorporated over time into larger towns and cities.

In Alberta, the first two German settlers are attested to in 1882. In 1891, German Lutherans from Galicia founded Hoffnungsau and Rosenthal (today Stony Plains) just west of Edmonton, while German Lutherans from Volhynia established their first settlements south of Edmonton, thus creating a "centre" of Volhynian Germans in Canada.

The first German towns in Saskatchewan (Strasburg, Edenwold and Langenburg) were founded by Protestant immigrants in 1885; in the following year, the colony of Josephstal near Balgonie was established by German Catholics from Russia. Starting in 1891, German Mennonites from Manitoba founded brother-colonies in northern Saskatchewan between the forks of the Saskatchewan River, with the town of Rosthern as a focal point. Mennonite immigrants from Ontario arrived in Alberta in 1893.

By 1890, German-Americans had also begun to move into Canada's West. Probably the most ambitious German-American settlement project between 1902 and 1905 was the founding of two German-language colonies in northern Saskatchewan by the Catholic Settlement Society of St. Paul: St. Peter's Colony had fifty townships, with Humboldt and Muenster as town centres, while St. Joseph's Colony boasted seventy-seven townships.

German-Americans established the first German colony in the Peace River area, the northernmost arable area of the settled part of Canada, in 1916.

BETWEEN THE WARS

Immigration between the wars occurred for the most part from 1923 to 1930; as in prewar years, German immigrants came mainly from eastern and southeastern European countries. From the Soviet Union, Volhynia, central Poland, Galicia and the Banat came people looking for freedom from discrimination and oppression. In 1923, Germans from Germany (*Reichsdeutsche*) were again admitted, and Canada proved to be as attractive as the United States for those immigrants. A number of them did move on to the United States, but there was also a substantial stream of German-American immigration to Canada (eighteen per cent of total German immigration) between the wars.

Although a number of Germans moved to Ontario and into larger cities such as Montréal, German settlements in western Canada were substantially reinforced by *Reichsdeutsche* settlers, German-Americans and the German refugees fleeing the Soviet Union after the Bolshevik revolution. The refugees from the Soviet Union were from a much broader social spectrum than the nineteenth-century German immigrants; German-language publications were to benefit greatly from the refugees' arrival in western Canada.

A distinct group of German immigrants are the Hutterites, an Anabaptist community that, like the Mennonites, emerged from the radical wing of the Protestant Reformation. They live in isolation from the world on communal farms called *Brüderhöfe* (colonies of Brethren), each having no more than 130 people.

Like the Mennonites and other German colonists, the Hutterites had been persuaded by Empress Catherine II to cultivate the territories of southern Russia depopulated and devastated by the Russo-Turkish wars, a task they promptly accomplished. However, large numbers of Anabaptists began to leave for the United States when, in 1870, the Tsar withdrew their privilege of peaceful neutrality and began to draft even the declared pacifists to military service. Between 1874 and 1877, three groups of Hutterian Brethren settled in the Dakotas.

During the First World War, the U.S. government kept its promise to the Hutterites of exemption from military service, but massive discrimination by the population at large prompted about fifty families to move up to Canada in 1918. These families founded the first Hutterite colonies in Manitoba and Alberta, where today most of them have settled although colonies of Hutterian Brethren continue to exist in South Dakota,

Montana and Saskatchewan. Of the more than twenty-five thousand North American Hutterites living in about 225 settlements, over seventy per cent live in Canada.

While the German-Russian and German-American immigration after the First World War considerably strengthened the German element in western Canada, the withdrawal of school privileges from German-speaking religious communities resulted in an exodus of Mennonites from Manitoba to Latin America. In 1922, about 3,300 Old Order Mennonites migrated from the West Reserve to northern Mexico in the vicinity of Chihuahua, and in 1926 about 1,200 Sommerfelder sect members from the East Reserve and about 150 from the West Reserve left for Paraguay.

In 1927, Germany was again declared a privileged country for immigration, which meant that not only German farmers but also skilled tradesmen and professionals were readily admitted. Consequently, the influx of German immigrants increased for a few years, but it nearly ceased altogether during the world economic crisis of 1931. Only a small group of German immigrants arrived in Canada in the late 1930s—about one thousand anti-Hitler Social Democrats from the Sudetenland, from all walks of life, settled as agriculturists in Saskatchewan and the Peace River area at Pouce Coupe, northern British Columbia. Only a very few individual political emigrants from Austria and Germany succeeded in immigrating to Canada before the Second World War.

AFTER THE SECOND WORLD WAR

Canada presented itself as an attractive proposition for impoverished postwar emigrants, above all for displaced and expelled European refugees. In the first twenty years after the war, 2.5 million people chose Canada as their new home. Between 1946 and 1971, more than 412,000 people from Germany, Austria and Switzerland immigrated. If one assumes that a full third of the immigrants returned to Europe—as German statistics suggest—then a net gain of 250,000 German immigrants can be registered for Canada within a period of roughly twenty-five years.

For German nationals, immigration to Canada was again permitted beginning in September 1950. This resulted in the mass immigration of Germans to Canada for the next twenty years, especially in the 1950s, but the flood declined to a trickle when Canadian immigration laws were changed in the 1970s.

Since the beginning of British colonization, the Germans have been Canada's third largest ethnic group after the British and the French, with a representation of between five and eight percent; in the West, they are the second largest ethnic group. In the 1951 census, 619,995 persons acknowledged German descent. The true figure, the experts agree, had to be several hundred thousand higher. The census of 1971 registered 1,317,195 people of German descent, of whom 561,000 listed German as their mother tongue and 219,350 as their most frequently used language of communication. These figures reveal a rapid process of assimilation, which, in turn, affects statistics on descent.

The results of the 1981 census are of particular interest. In this year the federal government abandoned its practice of requesting the nationality or language affiliation of immigrant ancestors, allowing instead two ethnic origins to be listed. By these criteria, the number of people of German stock rose to well above 1.7 million. In 1986, when an indication of multiple descent was permitted, the number of Canadians declaring German descent rose to almost 2.5 million.Comparing this figure with the number of persons still speaking German—according to the 1981 census, this amounts to about 150,000—the accelerated pace of assimilation becomes evident. Because Germans tend to lose their language, some within the first generation, spoken German in Canada has fallen from third to fourth place behind English, French and Italian.

The phenomenon of rapid assimilation accounts for the low visibility of German-Canadians; what should be stressed, however, is that this barely visible group of German immigrants has left clearly discernible evidence of many positive contributions to Canadian culture.

RELIGIOUS COMMUNITIES

Although German immigrants created a variety of secular organizations, it is difficult to overestimate the importance of religious institutions in the organization of communal life during the early pioneer period.

Of the German-speaking congregations, the **Mennonites** were the best off, for they always migrated in groups under the leadership of their elders or preachers. Features of their faith are adult baptism, the sanctity of marriage, nonintervention by the state in matters of faith and conscientious objection to military service.

The Mennonites flourished in the sixteenth century in Frisian lands, deriving their name from their founder, Menno Simons. Persecuted by both Roman Catholic and Protestant rulers alike, Mennonites found brief refuge in the Netherlands, in western Prussia and, after the Thirty Years' War, in southwest Germany and Moravia. In 1683, they started migrating to the United States, where they settled mainly in Pennsylvania; starting in 1788, after the Empress Catherine granted the privilege of peaceful neutrality, they also migrated to inhabit the empty wastelands of southern Russia. About fifteen thousand Mennonites left Russia between 1874 and 1879 after Russia introduced universal, compulsory military service; eight thousand went to the United States, and seven thousand came to Canada. These German-Russian Mennonites used the West-Prussian dialect as their common language.

Other Mennonites had migrated to Ontario from Pennsylvania as early as 1786. Of the Pennsylvania-German Mennonites who had originated in southwestern Germany, most spoke the dialect of the Palatinate region, which became "Pennsylfanish German" in the United States. They were followed by two more migratory waves from Russia after the Bolshevik revolution of 1917 and again after the Second World War. In the last two decades, many people have come to Canada from Mexico and Paraguay; they are descendants of those Old Order and Bergthaler Mennonites who left Manitoba for Latin America in the 1920s.

There are twenty-four different Mennonite groups in Canada, most of them in the West. A Mennonite characteristic is their steadfast adherence to their German mother tongue, which they have retained for many centuries on their migrations through four continents. Only the Amish subgroups of Swiss- and southern-German Old Order Mennonites, about four thousand people located mostly in Ontario, still use German both at church and in the home. Six other groups (with fifty-four congregations) of Old Order Mennonites of Low German descent, located mostly in western Canada, preserve their old ways in regard to dress, daily habits and the use of both High and Low German for their church services.

A number of more modern Mennonite groups switched to English-language church services in the 1950s; nevertheless, the Mennonite Brethren Church and the Conference of Mennonites in Canada still regularly offer German church services, from Ontario to British Columbia. According to the 1981 census, 189,370 Canadians, that is, almost eleven per cent of all persons of German descent, were Mennonites.

Also derived from the Anabaptist wing of the Reformation are the **Hutterites** or Hutterian Brethren (*Hutterer*), named after their Tyrolean founder, Jakob Hutter. There are about 17,000 in Canada, who use the German language in their religious services. Pacifism, adult baptism and the joint use of property mark their faith. The Hutterites thus practise a form of congregational communism, that is, life in a Christian commune. On their way through many countries, they have clung to their old-fashioned clothing, a regional costume worn in the sixteenth and seventeenth centuries in Moravia, as well as their native tongue, a Carinthian-Tyrolean dialect.

To practise their faith without harassment, the Hutterites left their native Germany and the German cantons of Switzerland, migrated to Moravia, escaped to the Hungarian parts of Slovakia and from there moved to Transylvania and Walachia. Some continued on to Russia in 1770. After the universal military draft in Russia in 1874, the Hutterites migrated to America, where they founded three *Brüderhöfe* in South Dakota.

Today, more than two-thirds of the 225 North American Hutterite colonies are in Alberta, Saskatchewan and Manitoba. These colonies, numbering between 75 and 130 people, are communes in matters of faith, economics and family. They are economically autonomous units, loosely confederated in an umbrella organization which holds annual meetings.

The German language did not survive in other German-Canadian religious congregations founded before the 1950s. This is particularly obvious in the case of the **Lutherans**, who, before the arrival of the Scandinavians, were a purely German church.

Wherever group immigration of Lutherans occurred, efforts were immediately made to organize a congregation and call for the appointment of a pastor. In Lunenburg, for example, a Lutheran congregation was founded soon after the town had been established; not until 1772, however, was a church built and a pastor appointed. The last German-speaking preacher there left office in 1897; he had been assisted by an English-speaking pastor since 1877. Similarly, Lutherans organized a congregation in Halifax immediately after their arrival there in 1750; in 1756, the schoolhouse was rebuilt into a church, consecrated in 1761 as St. George's. For lack of a pastor, services were conducted by schoolteachers; not until the arrival of the Loyalists did Halifax receive a German pastor, the only one ever appointed. After his death, St. George's congregation was absorbed by the Anglican church.

In eastern Ontario, the German Loyalists in Dundas and Stormont counties began construction of their first church a few years after their arrival. It was consecrated as Zion's Church in 1789 in Williamsburg. Congregations along the St. Lawrence mostly retained the Lutheran faith even after the change to English-language church services. The churches at the Bay of Quinte, on the other hand, became Methodist after switching to English.

The German Lutherans of Toronto merged into a single Lutheran congregation in 1851; to this day, it is known as the First Lutheran Church. Two years later, the German Lutheran St. John's congregation was founded in Montréal; it, too, still exists. The Lutheran congregations in Waterloo County date back to the endeavours of one pastor, Friedrich W. Bindemann. Pastor Bindemann, a Reformed Universalist, founded six congregations, among them St. Paul's in Kitchener (1835) and St. John's in Waterloo (1837).

The founding of Lutheran congregations in western Canada quickly followed the arrival of German settlers. The first Lutheran church of western Canada, the Trinity Church in Winnipeg, came into existence when Lutherans arrived from Bessarabia and Galicia in 1889. In 1897, the six pastors of the United Lutheran Church joined to found the Manitoba Synod. The Missouri Synod sent out its first pastor in 1894; he served as minister in Stony Plains from 1895, and this church spread fairly rapidly. The Ohio Synod, which started its mission in western Canada in 1905, was also very successful.

The Second World War caused big changes. Most German Lutheran congregations, with a few exceptions due to assistance directly from Germany, converted in the 1950s to English services. Although two-thirds of Lutherans in Canada are of German descent, the Lutheran Church here has made a clean break with its German past. The members of those bilingual congregations still remaining are postwar immigrants, in many instances *Volksdeutsche* from East European countries.

Roman Catholic Germans, most of whom began to arrive in southwestern Ontario in large numbers in the 1820s from southwest Germany, Alsace, Bavaria, Hesse and the Rhineland, faced much greater difficulties founding congregations than did the Mennonites and Lutherans. In most of the obviously German towns of southwestern Ontario, members of the three faiths settled side by side, although German Catholics gathered in large numbers in northeast Waterloo County (New Germany and vicinity), as well as west of Berlin (between Rummelhart and St. Agatha). Since the number of German Catholic congregations in Waterloo increased rapidly in the 1860s, the relatively few German priests (of whom most had been educated at St. Jerome's College, founded in St. Agatha and transferred to Berlin in 1886) could not minister to the Niagara German Catholics. These people turned for solace to congregations of Irish-Canadian Catholics. In Waterloo County itself, many German Catholic congregations, thinned by migration to the Huron Tract, became multinational.

The situation was different in western Canada. Governments and the railroad encouraged group settlement by ethnoreligious criteria; German Roman-Catholics were guided—with the assistance of German-Catholic migration associations—to Saskatchewan. The numerous congregations there were served by religious orders such as the Oblates and Benedictines and by German Catholic clergymen. German nuns also served in these congregations. Some were Ursuline sisters; others were of the Klagenfurt Order of St. Elizabeth. The nuns taught school classes or tended the sick in hospitals.

The People's Association for German-Canadian Catholics (*Volksverein für deutsch-kanadische Katholiken*) was founded in July 1909 in St. Joseph's Church, Winnipeg. By 1915 the association had fifty-five local branch units (*Ortsgruppen*) and at the end of the 1930s it still retained thirty-six, with four to five thousand members. The close link between church and association led to the establishment of many clubs within German-Catholic congregations, with many church buildings finding rooms for social club activities. All of the western Canadian congregations have now been fully assimilated, but the postwar immigration of Germans means that German-language services continue to be offered in Roman Catholic congregations in Vancouver (Holy Family), Calgary and Edmonton (St. Boniface), Winnipeg (St. Joseph's) and Toronto (St. Patrick's).

The North American **Baptist Church,** originally of purely German origin, today maintains twenty-one German-speaking congregations in Canada from British Columbia to Ontario. The history of German Baptist settlements in Canada begins with the group migration of Dobrudsha Germans (from Romania) to Saskatchewan in 1895.

Another originally German religious community is the **Moravian Church** (*Unitas Fratrum, Herrnhuter Brüdergemeinde*). The Moravian Brethren originated with the Reformation movement of Johannes Hus in Bohemia in the fifteenth century and received the distinguished patronage of Count Nikolaus von Zinzendorf on his estate at Herrnhut in Saxony (Germany). The North American centre of the Moravians is Bethlehem, Pennsylvania.

The German-Russian migration of Moravian Brethren to Canada began in 1892. The resulting settlements of Bruderheim (1895) and Heimtal (1896) are both near Edmonton. The Moravians, or Herrnhuter, are Pietists who at first adopted the Augsburg Confession, but then began to draw closer to the churches of Scotland and England. Since their relocation to Pennsylvania in the eighteenth century, the Moravians have begun to Anglicize.

Across Canada, German congregations no longer play the important role in ethnicity retention that they did before the Second World War. Today, their main activity is confined to city centres.

ACHIEVEMENTS AND CONTRIBUTIONS

What is more surprising than the numerically strong presence and rapid assimilation of Canada's third largest and nearly invisible ethnic group, however, is its level of achievement and the number of its contributions to this country's social and cultural mosaic. Because of the scarcity of coherent and detailed information on the German heritage in Canada, it is difficult to present a clear picture and evaluation of the whole of this heritage. German-Canadian studies is a new field of research, not systematized until 1972 when the Historical Society of Mecklenburg Upper Canada was founded in Toronto. Researchers on German Canadiana cannot, like German-American scholars, draw on a century or more of continuous data collection and analysis. For over two centuries, Canadian historians generally ignored our German heritage. Nonetheless, some important aspects of this heritage have come to the fore.

In 1936, for example, the *Encyclopedia of Canada*, edited by Stewart Wallace, was full of praise:

> The Germans are among the best immigrants; they are intelligent, honest, industrious, and thrifty; they make ideal farmers, and, in other walks of life, are good citizens. Although some of the German settlers are content with

the life as a labourer in the city, the majority are farmers. In the Lunenburg settlement they have become shipbuilders, sailors, and fishermen. The assimilation of the Germans to a Canadian nationality has made extensive, though not uniform progress.

In 1941, Watson Kirkconnell, the Canadian historian who was the first to trace the different ethnic groups in Canada systematically, wrote of the Germans, "Their contributions to Canadian life have been many and eminent." The *Encyclopedia Canadiana* of 1958 stresses the long tradition of German contributions to Canadian life:

> Canadians of German origin are the largest non-British, non-French stock in the population. Some arrived even before it had been decided whether Canada was to be French or British, others have been intimately connected with every later phase of settlement. ... As they pioneered in the settlement of Eastern Canada, so, too, German-speaking people pioneered in the opening of the West.

Among past historians who made general statements on the German heritage, there was a consensus that the main contribution was in the field of agriculture. To quote again the *Encyclopedia Canadiana* of 1958: "With good fortune or bad, farmers of German origin tended to remain farmers in Canada, participating in the general cityward drift far less and more slowly than other groups. In 1951, 64 % of Canadians of German origin in the West and 54 % of those in Eastern Canada were classified as rural." Although this percentage has changed drastically since 1951 in favour of the cities as a result of massive postwar immigration, it is true that the German contribution to Canadian agriculture has been outstanding.

Germans have pioneered as farmers in the Maritimes, Ontario and the West. Germans from Russia were the first to grow the now world-famous Canadian wheat in the Manitoba prairies, and Germans introduced viticulture in the Niagara Peninsula as well as fruit-growing to Nova Scotia's Annapolis Valley, now one of the leading fruit-producing areas in Canada. They also helped make the Okanagan Valley in British Columbia the chief fruit-growing area in western Canada. A number of individual Germans became well known for their record harvests and as developers of new brands of seed. In Manitoba, Walter Kroekes was called the potato king and Gerhard Elias the barley king. In British Columbia, Hermann Trelle, who won the world wheat championship five times for Canada, ranked for decades as the undisputed wheat king. By growing ever-more-resistant wheat varieties, Trelle attracted an increasing number of farmers to the Peace River region.

Next to the farmers it was the multitude of inventive German craftsmen who had an impact on Canadian society by helping to create a sound economic infrastructure wherever they settled. Although one can find general statements in the secondary literature claiming that Germans excelled primarily in furniture building, tanning, beer brewing, the rubber industry and textiles, a closer look reveals a much wider variety of ventures.

A good example can be found by a look into the economic history of Berlin/Kitchener. In the middle of the nineteenth century, with the strong influx of direct emigration from Germany, industry and commerce began to thrive in Berlin. A further impetus was given when, in 1856, the railway tracks reached the city. German immigrants there produced agricultural machines, ploughs, stoves, bricks, beer barrels, leather and textile items, buttons, shoes, boots, furniture, wood-processing machines, tools, jewellery, suitcases, bicycles, sports articles, cigars, gramophones, pianos and harmonicas, buildings and—of course—beer and sausages. Many of these plain immigrant craftsmen adapted to growing industrialization, and some became entrepreneurs of national, even international renown: Louis Breithaupt with his leather factories; Hartmann Krug with his furniture production; John Metz Schneider with his sausage business; the bootmaker Georg Rumpel, who became the felt king of Canada; and Jakob Kaufmann with his rubber companies, which reached such gigantic proportions that Kitchener has played the same role in Canada that Akron has played in the United States. Welker's gramophone production led to the worldwide Electrohome Industries; David Kuntz's private beer brewery eventually became Canada's largest trust, Carling Breweries Ltd; Reinhold Lang's tannery was for some time the largest in the British empire; and out of William Hespeler's schnapps distillery grew the now world-famous Seagram liquor imperium.

Berlin's first bank opened in 1853, and the first telegraph post was installed that same year. Import and export firms were founded, and Berlin's sister city, Waterloo, pioneered in the insurance business (Waterloo was sometimes called the Hartford of Canada). By the turn of the century, "Busy Berlin" was regarded as Canada's leading industrial town, but in one welcome feature it was unlike the industrial towns of other nations; when the Governor General was shown around the city, with its large percentage of workers, he was surprised to find no slums.

Berlin was one of the first Canadian cities to hold an industrial exhibition, arranged and organized by the German-Canadian Music and Choir Association of the Concordia Club in 1905. Premier J.P. Whitney opened the exhibition with the following words: "Today, Berlin stands at the head of the procession in the Dominion. Such an occasion has never been known before in Canada. I will tell people to come here for lessons in enterprise and progress."

It was a symbol of Berlin's leading role in Ontario's industrialization that the city was the first, in October 1910, to benefit from electricity generated by the Niagara Falls. The Hydro-Electric Power Commission of Ontario, which was responsible for this achievement, had been conceived by two Berlin businessmen, E.W.B. Snider and D.B. Detweiler, and put into practice by Adam Beck, a native of the village of Baden near Berlin, who, as minister without portfolio, had introduced a bill in 1906 to create this huge organization.

Some outstanding examples demonstrate the wide scope of German entrepreneurial spirit. Samuel Zimmermann, a German who emigrated from Pennsylvania to Thorold on the Niagara Peninsula, constructed part of the Welland Canal, and built part of the Great Western and other Ontario railway lines as well as a suspension bridge and a railway bridge across the Niagara River. When he was killed at the age of forty-two in a mysterious railway accident, he was regarded as the richest man in Canada. Looking at Toronto's past, it is noteworthy that Canada's leading piano factory was founded in the nineteenth century by Theodor Heintzmann, and the earliest music shops by S. Nordheimer. More recently, during the last thirty years or so, not only did a considerable number of manufacturing and construction firms founded by German-Canadians grow to sizeable proportions in Toronto, but some food-producing firms acquired regional, even national importance, such as Bittner's chain of meat shops and the bread factories of Dimpflmayer and Paech (Rudolph's Bakery).

In the economic history of western Canada, one might mention Alvo von Alvensleben, a Prussian nobleman who, around 1910, was the most famous real-estate broker in Vancouver. Alfred von Hammerstein, after the turn of the century, was the first to exploit Alberta's Athabasca oil sands on a large scale. The Austrian-born Karl F. Landegger founded the Prince Albert Paper Company, which is now regarded as the largest industrial enterprise in Saskatchewan. For Manitoba, one could mention a number of Mennonite business success stories; it may suffice to refer to the astonishing economic development of the town of Steinbach, a phenomenon that parallels Berlin's rise in the nineteenth century.

It is often alleged that Germans played no role in Canadian politics. This is probably true with regard to group voting and lobbying; only rarely did the Germans exert group pressure on a regional or provincial level, as in the famous school controversies in Waterloo County and Manitoba. They never applied group pressure on a national level. As individuals, however, people of German descent or origin participated in public life on all levels. Three of the Fathers of Confederation were of German descent: Charles Tupper of Nova Scotia, who became prime minister in 1896; Charles Fisher; and William Henry Steeves (originally Stief) of New Brunswick. German names can be found among provincial deputies in Nova Scotia, New Brunswick, Quebec, Ontario,

Manitoba, Alberta and British Columbia. Some German-Canadians served as cabinet members in their respective provincial governments. For four generations, members of the prominent Breithaupt family of Kitchener held various public offices, with L.O. Breithaupt serving as lieutenant-governor of Ontario from 1952 to 1956. In Alberta, Horst Schmid from Bavaria became the first postwar immigrant to rise to the rank of cabinet minister; a more recent arrival is Frank Oberle from British Columbia. John Diefenbaker, who was of German and Scottish descent, became prime minister in 1957, and Edward Schreyer, whose ancestors were Germans from Galicia (Poland) and whose relatives currently reside in the Federal Republic of Germany, became governor general in 1978, the first German-Canadian to hold this post.

German-Canadians have excelled in science, education, architecture, painting, sculpture and literature, as well as other intellectual and aesthetic endeavours. We would like to single out three other fields in which they have left a mark on Canadian society, the first two most obvious to the historian, the third more noticeable to the public at large: religion, music and folklore.

As pointed out, several religious denominations have been imported into Canada by Germans—Lutheranism, Methodism, the Mennonite, Amish, Hutterite and Moravian churches, and a few smaller sects such as the Tunkers or Dunkers. In addition to their work as ministers, many of the pioneer parsons had to be colonizers, organizers and teachers. Thus, they often played an important role in the founding and stabilization of new settlements.

The contributions made by German-Canadians to the development of musical life are disproportionate to their numerical strength. Many of Canada's leading musical institutions have been initiated by German-speaking people: the Société harmonique de Québec by Friedrich Glackemayer; the Toronto Symphony Orchestra by Luigi Maria von Kunits; the Winnipeg Philharmonic Society by Joseph Hecker; and the Atlantic Symphony Orchestra in Halifax by Robert Dietz. Augustus Stephen Vogt founded the Toronto Mendelssohn Choir, and Hermann Geiger-Torel, sometimes called Mr. Opera, came from Frankfurt, Germany, and succeeded in raising the Toronto-based Canadian Opera Company to an internationally acclaimed institution. Male choir singing was brought to Canada by Germans. The first German-Canadian musical society was founded as early as 1861 in Victoria, British Columbia, and went by the name of the Germania Singing Society; the Waterloo *Liedertafel* flourished between 1865 and the First World War. German-Canadian *Sängerfeste* (singers' festivals) started in Berlin, Ontario, during the last quarter of the nineteenth century. The largest *Sängerfest*, in 1886, lasted for three days and had seventeen choirs participating from Canada and the United States,

comprising 1,125 singers. Besides many other selections, the Berlin (Ontario) Philharmonic Orchestra Society, founded and conducted by Herman Theodore Zoellner, performed Joseph Haydn's oratorio *The Creation*, a major artistic challenge.

Several Canadian pioneer musicologists have come from Germany and Austria, such as the Viennese Ida Halpern, a specialist in the music of British Columbia's native people; the Berlin-born Ulrich Leopold, an expert in Lutheran church music; and Helmut Kallmann, who wrote the first *History of Music in Canada, 1534–1914* and who has been the director of the Music Division of the National Library of Canada, Ottawa, for many years. Moving from religion and classical music to the more popular field of folklore, one should, nevertheless, not underestimate the harmonizing effect of popular customs shared by many different segments of the population. By sharing pleasant experiences, the members of a multicultural society draw closer together without the anxieties of a distrustful ethnocentricity. As a result of two world wars, Germans have suffered from discrimination and a very one-sided coverage in the mass media; their descendants must be proud that Canadian society has readily accepted two German imports in the field of merrymaking, namely the *Karneval* or *Fasching*—a kind of Mardi Gras—and the Munich-style Oktoberfest. Kitchener-Waterloo's Oktoberfest, established in the 1950s by the twin cities' German clubs, is famous, and its organizers claim that its size is rivalled only by the original Munich festival itself.

In summary, German-Canadians are vigorous participants in all endeavours of Canadian life. Although they are, as one Canadian journalist has pointed out, "almost painfully unassertive," they are also "the least controversial, the least quarrelsome and least quarrelled-over in our whole society." Innovative, productive and creative, German-Canadians have contributed much to Canada, from early colonization to modern technology.

BIBLIOGRAPHY

Andre, John. *William Berczy, Co-Founder of Toronto*. Toronto: Borough of York, 1967.

Bausenhart, Werner. *German Immigration and Assimilation in Ontario, 1783–1918*. Ottawa and Toronto: LEGAS, 1989.

Bell, Winthrop P. *The "Foreign Protestants" and the Settlement of Nova Scotia*. Toronto: University of Toronto Press, 1961.

Bird, Michael, and Terry Kobayashi. *A Splendid Harvest: Germanic Folk and Decorative Art in Canada*. Toronto: Van Nostrand Reinhold, 1981.

Bovay, Emile H. *Le Canada et les Suisses,* 1604–1974. Fribourg: Edition Universitaires, 1976.

Epp, Frank H. *Mennonites in Canada, 1786–1920: The History of a Separate People.* Toronto: Macmillan, 1974.

———. *Mennonites in Canada, 1920–1940: A People's Struggle for Survival.* Toronto: Macmillan, 1982.

Friesen, Gerhard, and Karin Guerttler, eds. *German-Canadian Yearbook.* Vols. 8–10. Toronto: Historical Society of Mecklenburg Upper Canada, 1984–1988.

Froeschle, Hartmut, ed. *German-Canadian Yearbook.* Vols. 1–7. Toronto: Historical Society of Mecklenburg Upper Canada, 1973–1983.

Froeschle, Hartmut. *The History and Heritage of German Immigration to Canada.* Canadian Germanica. Occasional Papers, 3. Toronto: German-Canadian Historical Association, 1982.

Froeschle, Hartmut, and Lothar Zimmermann. *German Canadiana: A Bibliography.* Vol. 11, German-Canadian Yearbook. Toronto: Historical Society of Mecklenburg Upper Canada, 1990.

Gingerich, Orland. *The Amish of Canada.* Waterloo: Conrad Press, 1972.

Hostetler, John A., and G.E. Huntingdon. *The Hutterites in North America.* Toronto: Holt, Rinehart and Winston, 1967.

Kalbfleisch, Herbert. *The History of the Pioneer German Language Press of Ontario, 1835–1918.* Toronto: University of Toronto Press, 1968.

Lee-Whiting, Brenda. *Harvest of Stones: The German Settlement in Renfrew County.* Toronto: University of Toronto Press, 1985.

Lehmann, Heinz. *The German Canadians, 1750–1937: Immigration, Settlement and Culture.* Trans., ed. and introd. Gerhard P. Bassler. St. John's, 1986.

Leibbrandt, Gottlieb. *Little Paradise: The Saga of the German Canadians of Waterloo County, Ontario, 1800–1975.* Trans. G.K. Weissenborn. Kitchener: Allprint Co., 1980.

Lowell, Edgar J. *The Hessians and Other German Auxiliaries of Great Britain in the Revolutionary War.* Port Washington, N.Y.: Kennikal Press, 1965.

Mayer, Elizabeth M. *Stories About People of German Language Background in Victoria,* B.C. Victoria, 1986.

Ramsay, Bruce. *A History of the German-Canadians in British Columbia.* Vancouver: Alpen Club, 1958.

Reaman, G. Elmore. *The Trail of the Black Walnut.* Toronto: McClelland and Stewart, 1968.

Riedel, Walter E., ed. *The Old World and the New: Literary Perspectives of German-Speaking Canadians.* Toronto: University of Toronto Press, 1984.

Staebler, Edna L.C. *Food That Really Schmecks: Mennonite Country Cooking.* Toronto: McGraw-Hill Ryerson, 1968.

von Riedesel, Friederike C.L. *Baroness von Riedesel and the American Revolution: Journal and Correspondence of a Tour of Duty, 1776–1783.* Ed. and trans. M.L. Brown Jr. and Marta Huth. Chapel Hill: University of North Carolina Press, 1965.

Wilhelmy, Jean-Pierre. *Les mercenaires allemands au Québec du XVIIIe siècle et leur apport à la population.* Belœil, Quebec: Maison des Mots, 1984.